THE SHADOWS RISE

THE SHADOWS RISE

Abraham Lincoln and the Ann Rutledge Legend

John Evangelist Walsh

UNIVERSITY OF ILLINOIS PRESS
Urbana and Chicago

First Illinois paperback, 2009
© 1993 by the Board of Trustees
of the University of Ilinois

Manufactured in the United States of America
1 2 3 4 5 C P 5 4 3 2 1

∞ This book is printed on acid-free paper.

The Library of Congress cataloged the cloth edition as follows:
Walsh, John Evangelist, 1927–
The shadows rise: Abraham Lincoln and the Ann Rutledge legend /
John Evangelist Walsh.
p.   cm.
Includes bibliographical references and index.
ISBN 0-252-02011-1 (cl)
1. Lincoln, Abraham, 1809–1865—Friends and associates.
2. Rutledge, Ann, d. 1835. I. Title.
E457.35.W185   1993
973.7'092'2—dc20   92-34284
CIP

PAPERBACK ISBN 978-0-252-07629-9

O Memory! thou midway world
 'Twixt earth and Paradise,
Where things decayed and loved ones lost
 In dreamy shadows rise,

And, freed from all that's earthly vile,
 Seem hallowed, pure, and bright,
Like scenes in some enchanted isle
 All bathed in liquid light.

—From a poem by Abraham Lincoln
published May 5, 1847, in the
Quincy (Illinois) *Whig*

For
BILL AND MANDY
with love and
all best wishes

Contents

Acknowledgments

Several kind people have in various ways made my task easier with this book, and to them I return my sincerest thanks:

Thomas F. Schwartz, curator, the Lincoln Collection, Illinois State Historical Library, Springfield; Ruth Cook, the Lincoln Library and Museum, Fort Wayne, Indiana; the staff of the Manuscripts Division, Pelletier Library, Alleghany College, Meadville, Pennsylvania.

John C. Walsh, George Mason University, Virginia; Marjory B. Hinman, Broome County Historical Society, Binghamton, New York; Minerva Flagg, Windsor, New York; Clark Evans, Rare Books Division, Library of Congress.

Timothy A. Walsh, University of Wisconsin, Madison; Richard S. Taylor, chief of Technical Services, Historical Sites Division, Illinois Historic Preservation Society, Springfield; Aileen Altig, New Salem State Historic Site; Martin Gallas, Illinois College, Jacksonville.

Douglas L. Wilson, Knox College, Galesburg, Illinois; John Y. Simon, Southern Illinois University; James T. Hickey, curator (ret.), Lincoln Collection, Springfield; Dr. Paul M. Bancroft, Lincoln, Nebraska; William Beard, the Lincoln Legal Papers, Springfield; the staff of the Wisconsin State Historical Library, Madison; Lynda Bourquin and Maggie Guralski of the Arabut Ludlow Memorial Library, Monroe, Wisconsin.

My considerable debt to all the many able and conscientious scholars and writers of earlier years who tried sincerely to get at the truth about Abe and Ann may be read in the notes and the bibliography. I wish to thank them all, everyone on both sides of the question as well as those who preferred to remain in the middle, for making my own studies not alone stimulating but rewarding. Particularly I desire to offer to the

shade of William H. Herndon full recognition of my indebtedness—
and the indebtedness of all who write on the pre-presidential Lincoln—to
his wonderfully able and energetic (it were ungracious at this point to
dwell on its flaws) pioneering research.

THE SHADOWS RISE

Prologue: Ghost Town

WALKING ALONE down the middle of the pebbled road, I gazed at the ragged line of weathered log cabins that ran for a quarter-mile or so along either side. Spaced at random intervals, separated by rail fences, partially obscured by trees and bushes, there arose some twenty such structures, large and small. One building, nearly at the end on the right and set back from the road, was slightly larger than the rest. This, as my map indicated, was the Rutledge tavern.

Admiring the cozy neatness of the log construction, I continued to where the road bent a bit to the left, then I stopped and took several steps to my right. Reaching up, I pushed open the rough door of a medium-sized cabin bearing a sign that announced it as a grocery or general store. Inside, standing to the immediate right, was a rude, hip-high counter backed by a row of shelves. Around two of the other walls also ran shelves laden with goods, and built into the rear wall was a large, open fireplace with a small wooden bench set invitingly before it. If young Abe Lincoln's questing spirit ever chanced to wander in here, I thought, and if he didn't peer too closely at the merchandise, he could go right back to work behind the counter and feel very much at home.

The restored village of New Salem, though not large in extent, must be among the country's most impressive examples of meticulous and loving restoration. Situated some twenty miles northwest of Springfield, Illinois, the new village occupies much the same ground as the original. In layout and extent, and in the siting, construction, and identification of the individual buildings, all is as exact as careful study could make it. The furniture and artifacts in the cabins have been described as perhaps "the finest and most comprehensive collection of early American and pioneer relics ever assembled." Based on remarkably minute research (down to the differences in cabin construction between southerners and northerners), the lengthy effort at reconstruction was delayed almost too long, not starting until nearly every vestige of Lincoln's New Salem had disappeared (its life in any case was short, hardly a decade). All that remained for guidance were some of the filled-in cellar and foundation holes—by then covered with sixty years and more of overgrowth—and the memories of a few old settlers and their families.

The reconstructed village (the only whole village, apparently, ever erected as a memorial to one man) was surely worth the effort, for it is no exaggeration to say that frontier New Salem was the single most important place in which Abraham Lincoln ever lived. Here he ceased being a simple backwoodsman with axe constantly in hand and began the rapid and remarkable change that was to make him a leading intellect of his time, and one of history's most gifted statesmen. For the young and eager but still raw and untried Lincoln, New Salem provided that necessary moratorium in life, a safe retreat, in which he could try at his leisure just how he might fit into the world at large. As one scholar put it, New Salem was Lincoln's alma mater. Whether it was also the place where, through the bitter experience of a doomed love affair, he found how a man's heart itself may be changed—may be crushed and perhaps broken, never to heal—is a question often asked, and never yet finally answered.

For six years, Lincoln lived at New Salem, from ages twenty-two to twenty-eight, from July 1831 to mid-April 1837. During that time, his rustic neighbors knew him best not alone for his intelligence, or for his burgeoning leadership abilities, but for something much more humanly appealing. To these plain people Lincoln was simply the best-natured, most companionable, most all-around interesting, capable, and likeable young man they had ever met. That undoubted fact, easily lost sight of in the press of later events, is important to recall, for the truth is that Lincoln began his rise to fame because of it. As was said by his long-time law partner William Herndon (who will play a major role in these pages), Lincoln "never saw the minute, the hour, nor the day when he did not have many financial friends to aid him, and to help him in all ways. His friends vied with each other for the pleasure or the honor of assisting him. . . . Lincoln was the favorite of everybody—man, woman, and child—where he lived and was known, and he richly deserved it." Herndon also reports Lincoln's own admission that it was at New Salem that he first began, though vaguely, to dream of a destiny.

Here he first applied himself to more settled occupations, earning his living as grocery clerk, postmaster, and surveyor, all positions voluntarily offered him by his friends, and at odd times still acting as farmhand, woodchopper, rail-splitter, and once as tender of a whiskey still. A reputation for an agile tongue was also quickly gained, both as a teller of humorous stories among his cronies and as a speaker before large crowds, two rare talents that, though related, do not always come together in the same man.

Also—and in this frontier society by no means least—he soon became known as a man of prodigious physical strength as well as fine athletic ability, both of which he was often called on to demonstrate. Aside from contests in running, jumping, and wrestling, a favorite exhibition was to load a wooden platform with rocks, as much as a thousand pounds, which Lincoln would lift from the ground by means of a harness strapped over his shoulders. When Joshua Speed of Springfield, later his closest friend, first heard of Lincoln from the New Salemites it was precisely because of this Paul Bunyanesque quality: "I heard him spoken of by those who knew him as a wonderful character. They boasted that he could outwrestle any man in the county, and that he could beat any lawyer in Springfield in speaking."

Perhaps the best sign of the special and even unique position Lincoln rapidly achieved in the New Salem community is this: running in his first election for the state legislature, only a year after he arrived a stranger in town, out of the 300 votes cast in his own precinct he received an astonishing 277. Being unknown in the other precincts, he lost that election, but two years later he succeeded: as one of four representatives chosen from Sangamon County out of a slate of thirteen, he ran second, coming within four votes of the top. At the next election, that of 1836, he was chosen first among seventeen candidates.

Of all the many log houses in the reconstructed New Salem, the one that held particular interest for me was the Rutledge tavern. Only a two-minute walk from the Lincoln grocery, it sat well back from the pebbled road, with an air of solidity or quality that seemed lacking in some of the other buildings. Its ground floor, I saw on entering, held two rooms, both fairly large, the main one serving as a kitchen-dining-living area. The other was a sleeping-sitting room, holding several beds, big and little, most with trundles underneath. The two-part loft, where Lincoln himself often bedded down, could hold any number of over-nighters rolled in blankets on the bare floor or on the usual hay mattresses.

As I stood in the tavern's main room, looking around at the rough-made yet curiously comfortable furniture, I tried to think myself back to the early 1830s. Ann, the Rutledges' eldest daughter, would often have been here then, spending a good part of every day amid the noisy talk at the long table and the mingled aromas of roasting meats and baking bread. She would have helped her mother with the cooking at the large open fireplace, perhaps also assisting in serving the several guests, all of them probably remaining for only a night or two on their busy way to some other place.

The youthful Lincoln, too, had often been in the original of this room, had for a while lodged at the tavern, had many, many times met and spoken with Ann. Had the two really been deeply in love, as the now familiar legend would have it, actually engaged to marry? Had Ann's tragic death when she was only twenty-two pushed the grieving Lincoln to the edge of a breakdown, of actual insanity? Had it inspired him to begin his climb to the political heights, making Ann, as was said by one of Lincoln's later friends, "one of the agents of destiny in the salvation and regeneration of the nation"? Or was the story nothing but some wild excess of the popular imagination, as has been maintained, based on a few or no facts, in reality "pure fiction"? Such questions, when asked about the man who was a principal architect of the modern age and who acted at the center of perhaps the most wrenching and pivotal political situation of the last five hundred years, are by no means trivial.

For a century and a third the argument about Abe and Ann has been with us, boiling or simmering, rising and falling in public interest according to circumstance. The popular mind, ever impatient over nice points of evidence, happily embraces and cherishes the notion of a great but doomed romance. Conscientious historians, on the other hand, most of them, plod along in the rear determinedly shaking their heads in dour disagreement. The last fifty years, in particular, have seen the Rutledge legend reduced by the experts to what is probably its minimal scholarly acceptance, and there is erosion even at the popular level. There have been moments, indeed, when the old tale has seemed at last hovering on the brink, liable to survive only as a sentimental myth, if at all, and recognized as such. But that sort of inglorious end, I had long felt, would be a pity, especially since the legend's sources had never been accorded a full and fair hearing.

Not the least surprising aspect of the Lincoln-Rutledge question, as it has existed up to now, is the absence of any sort of sustained investigation. Continually talked about and argued over in magazines, newspapers, and parts of books (surprisingly, the present volume is the first book-length investigation of the topic), it still can be said with perfect justice that the Rutledge legend in its full extent today stands largely unanalyzed, and very nearly unapproached. Closest to being a thoroughgoing professional study, and presently accounted most authoritative, was the 1945 effort by James G. Randall, who in his masterful study of the Lincoln presidency included an appendix on the Rutledge legend. In it he rendered a subtly negative judgment that readily convinced—as it also greatly satisfied—the bulk of his colleagues and other concerned readers, while apparently disappointing only a few.[*]

Randall denied to the legend all "intrinsic importance," thereby dismissing the possibility of any lasting or significant effect on Lincoln, even if the love story itself were true. While masses of documents went into his careful and dispassionate study, in his presentation he covered only the essence of the matter, ignoring the intermediate stages. "To spin out the analysis into an extended account," he explained, "would in the writer's view not alter the conclusion." This of course is a most curious way to write history, yet in Randall's case it has worked. Since Randall, professional historians in general have not, for a variety of reasons—some obvious, some not, some defensible, some not—really cared to give the Ann Rutledge episode too close scrutiny.

Leaving the Rutledge tavern, I walked on down the road to where it swung left among the trees. As I went I passed several cabins on the right belonging to families by the names of Alley, Whary, Camron, and Herndon (a cousin of William), all of them, as I knew, friends of the young Lincoln. Pausing at the Herndon cabin I peered in through the door, for here (in the original cabin) had taken place a shocking event

---

[*]Two articles, by the historians John Y. Simon and Douglas Wilson, both published in 1990, raise quite effective challenges to Randall. They are treated in chapter 3.

involving the death of Herndon's wife, which I felt sure must have concerned Lincoln. As it happened, I eventually came across a document showing a fleeting connection between him and the incident, and though it was a small thing, it still threw a momentary light on one day in the legend, affording one of the very few authentic glimpses of Abe and Ann together.

After a short stroll, the road led me to the bluff overlooking the Sangamon River, where stood the small rough-built grocery store in which Lincoln had clerked for Denton Offut when he first reached New Salem. The open ground beside this store, supposedly, is where Lincoln fought that memorable wrestling bout with Jack Armstrong. To my eye, however, as I looked around at the narrow strip of bluff, there didn't seem to be nearly enough room at that spot for the epic struggle, witnessed as it was by a thronging crowd of cheering onlookers.

Turning, I walked back along the village's main street (its only street, if one or two short spurs may be discounted), soon coming abreast of another store that Lincoln had operated in New Salem. This was the shop he had owned in partnership with William Berry, the one that had steadily failed during some six months until at last, in Lincoln's own wry phrase, it had "winked out." Along the store's narrow front was attached a plain covered porch, with a bench hugging the wall. Sitting down on the bench, I let my gaze roam out over the captivatingly authentic scene presented up and down the road, at length coming to rest on the Rutledge tavern directly across from me.

As I stared at the sturdy new-old structure, I again called up the picture of a very real Ann busily tending her household chores, a bright, pretty, charmingly amiable young woman, as all who knew her readily testified. I saw her there with her blondish or light sandy hair and smiling blue eyes, surrounded by her large and close-knit family, all of them mercifully unaware that shortly she would be dead, none ever dreaming that so strange—and strangely variable—an immortality awaited her.

It was time, I decided as I looked at the gray, weathered walls of the tavern, for someone to make that sustained examination of her legend, to "spin out" to its full length the whole complex story of Abe and Ann. It was time to see if the truth, or any significant portion of it, after the passage of almost a hundred and sixty years was still recoverable.

A patient reconstruction of the entire story would be needed, its start, its growth, its impact. The actual evidence in the case, all of it both for and against, must be gathered, analyzed, presented. For this, so far as possible, I must work with original documents, and, luckily, the most important of these were ready to hand in one location. At the Library of Congress, I knew, reposed the firsthand testimony of more than twenty men and women of old New Salem, all well known to Abe and Ann. Whatever else might turn up, it seemed clear, according to the recollections of these privileged witnesses the legend must survive or fall.

1

Discovering Ann

AT SUNRISE on a wooded bluff high above the Sangamon River, a lone figure paused in his walk to take a seat on a rough boulder. At this early hour on the exposed bluff the air was raw and cold, but the man was too preoccupied to notice. For some minutes he sat listening to two muted but sharply contrasting sounds—the subdued hum of the river, not quite a roar, as it poured over the milldam at the foot of the bluff, and the dull leaden tinkle of a distant cowbell. As he listened, his alert, blue eyes slowly swept the open ground, flanked by thick forest, that stretched away from him toward the west. Shortly, his flitting gaze came to rest on the sole man-made structure in view, a log cabin in the clearing off to his left.

Fronting north, the lone cabin was one story high with a loft on top. It had two doors at ground level and presumably two rooms, but it was obviously not in good condition. Its ancient roof was mostly tumbled in, and each of the gables, while still supporting the remains of a chimney, had begun to crumble.

From his pocket the man took a notebook and pencil, balancing the notebook on his knee. A blank page he headed with the date Monday, October 15, 1866, then he jotted down the location and condition of the cabin, adding, "Abraham has been in it probably a hundred times." The man was William Henry Herndon, surviving member of the law firm of Lincoln & Herndon. On this morning he had reached the crux of the task he had set himself only the year before, and from which he would not be free for the rest of his days. The ruined cabin had once been the busy Rutledge tavern of vanished New Salem. Inside its walls, Herndon was convinced, had begun the love-tragedy which, if properly understood, would explain all that was mysterious or puzzling in the life and personality of his slain partner.

As the sun, brightly climbing above the trees on the far side of the river, began burning off the morning fog, Herndon turned to look south. The view along the curving river, as he duly entered in his notebook, presented a series of low, mist-shrouded ridges rising gently one behind the other, all softly clothed in melting shades of dark blues and greens and muted orange. Swinging around to peer north, he encountered the same general scene, though it was "not so grand, because less distinct and prominent to the eye." Then, standing up, he resumed his walk.

Heading down into a long, narrow gully at the side of the clearing, he crossed a sluggish stream, clambered over moss-draped boulders, then worked his way up again onto the level. As he went he noticed the bare trees and saw how the few leaves on the denuded branches "hung dry, curled and quivering." At intervals he paused to enter in his notebook brief descriptions of the landscape—huge glacier-strewn rocks embedded in the hillside, one of which had "the look, smell, and feel of fire on it." The multitude of flowers at his feet he took time to list by name: purple aster, blue lobelia, yellow acacia, primrose. He noted the standing timber as being the usual elm, sycamore, cottonwood, and maple, and he especially observed that there was little or no game to be seen, at least none of the turkey, quail, and deer that had once been so abundant.

After his unhurried stroll, he came back to his rocky seat on the bluff and once more he let his eyes trail pensively over and across the open ground stretching before him. "As I sat on the verge of the town in the presence of its ruins," he wrote in the notebook on his knee, "I called to mind the street running east and west through the village. . . . I cannot exclude from my memory or imagination the forms, faces, voices and features of those I once knew so well. In my imagination, the little village perched on the hill is astir with the hum of busy men, and the sharp, quick buzz of women." In his memory he saw men and women, afoot and on horseback, coming to town from the surrounding countryside, "to see and to be seen; to hear and to be heard; to barter and to exchange what they have with the merchant and the laborer." The names of some of the people who had been part of the bustling little village he had no trouble recalling, people he had known in his own youth and some of whom were still living: William Green, Jack Kelso, James Short, Caleb Carman, Sam Hill, John McNamar, Jason Duncan, Jacob Bale, Jack Armstrong, Mentor Graham. "Oh, how sad and solemn are New Salem's memories to me," he finished. "The spirit of the place to me is lonely and yet sweet. It presides over the soul gently, tenderly." Thinking particularly of the two principals in the drama he was trying so meticulously to reconstruct, he added feelingly, "May the spirits of the loved and loving dead here meet and embrace, as was denied them on earth."

By the fall of 1866, Abraham Lincoln had lain in his temporary Springfield tomb for some fifteen months. During almost that same length of time, William Herndon, in preparation for a planned biography, had been busily engaged in studying and researching nearly every aspect of the dead man's past. Forty-eight years old, and one of Springfield's best-known figures, having been in steady partnership with Lincoln for sixteen years, Herndon had already gained some reputation as a Lincoln biographer. It had come, however, by means of the spoken, not the written word.

In a series of three lectures, delivered at Springfield and widely quoted in papers around the country, Herndon had supplied a fascinated public with an insider's view of the late president's character. Enjoying a unique access to people's confidence because of his privileged link with his subject, during those fifteen months he had diligently pursued the record of Lincoln's early life, even to the extent of badly neglecting his own law practice. In Illinois and Indiana, he visited sites that were closely connected with Lincoln's youth, talking with survivors who had known the young Lincoln, including one memorable session with the president's aged stepmother. It was in his own backyard, however, principally the town of Petersburg, that he had uncovered what promised to be among the most important, certainly the most intriguing, information of all. It concerned a part of Lincoln's life then unknown to the public, an old romance that had ended tragically, leaving what seemed to be a permanent scar on the young Lincoln's sensitive spirit.

Before starting his researches, Herndon had known nothing of this bygone love story. He had come across it almost by accident, in interviews and correspondence with some old New Salemites—in bits and pieces, out of the fragmented memories of a score of elderly men and women, it had arisen almost of its own volition. As fact, or what appeared to be fact, was added to fact, Herndon began to recognize the true significance of the old affair, or what he took to be the true significance. Almost jubilantly, he saw, or thought he saw, how it clarified much that had always seemed strange or inexplicable in his old partner. Convinced that he had stumbled on a major historical discovery, he soon decided he would not wait for completion of his biography of Lincoln but would make the story public immediately, in its main features at least. Another lecture with its attendant wide publicity seemed the obvious method, and his suggestion of a fall 1866 date had been quickly accepted by the same institution that had hosted his three previous talks, Springfield's Practical Business College.* His mid-October visit to the desolate site of old New Salem, besides fueling him emotionally for his task, gave him an up-to-the-minute portrait of the area as a frame for what he had begun to think of as "one of the world's most classic stories."

The talk that the large audience at the business college heard on the evening of November 16 lasted some three hours. A competent and apparently at times a highly effective speaker, Herndon was also known in town as being a strangely impulsive and often unpredictable personality. But he also possessed something of the true instinct of the born platform performer, and the lecture he had put together for this occasion—though in its printed form seeming woefully disjointed— strongly gripped his listeners' attention throughout the evening (helped, no doubt, by the newspaper's stressing that the talk was based on "records accessible to but few"). The title he gave it, and by which it had been advertised in advance, while awkward, still managed to exude an enticing air of revelation: "Abraham Lincoln, Miss Ann Rutledge, New Salem, Pioneering, and *The* Poem." Even his opening words, curiously abrupt, would have electrified the audience in the small auditorium, many of them Lincoln's personal friends and neighbors. In almost pell-mell fashion his thoughts tumbled out:

---

*Just at that time Springfield was in a mood for Lincoln revelations. Less than two weeks before Herndon's lecture, the actress Laura Keene was in town playing *Our American Cousin* on tour. The papers reported good attendance but failed to mention what, if anything, took place at the start of the third act, the moment when Booth had pulled the trigger.

Lincoln loved Ann Rutledge better than his own life; and I shall give the history of the poem so far as to connect it with the two in its own proper place and time. The facts in relation to Abraham, Ann and the poem, making a complete history, lie in fragments in the desk at my office, in the bureau drawers at my home, and in my memory.... This lecture is but a part—a *small* part—of a long, thrilling and eloquent story. I have not here told the whole story; nay, not the half of it; nor can I do so here understandingly, for the want of time. I am forced to keep something back from necessity, which shall, in due time, assume a more permanent form. That which is withheld is just as interesting, and more lovely, than I can here tell or relate.

He was making these revelations now, he said, to ensure that they would survive on the record should anything happen to him, for no one else so well understood "the many delicate wheels and hidden springs" of the story of Lincoln and Ann Rutledge. Such facts were indispensable to a clear picture of Mr. Lincoln's life, and he had no right to keep them "in my own selfish bosom any longer." Knowing well that the revelation he was about to make would inevitably be challenged, he abruptly insisted—in a remark that must have doubled the suspense already felt by the audience—that he was "willing that my character among you may stand or fall by the substantial truthfulness of this lecture." There was a pause, and then with marked emphasis he finished, *"in every particular."*

In deciding to present his audience that night with only an outline of the story, reserving full treatment for the biography, Herndon had complicated matters for himself. In abbreviated form the story of Abe and Ann was not nearly sufficient to fill a talk of two hours, hardly one. The problem had been solved, however, by providing the main story with a backdrop, folding it into a more generalized portrait of Lincoln's New Salem, "its men and times." The result, inevitably, was a hodgepodge of topics, though Herndon was able to smooth things over and keep his listeners' attention by the way he gave first a bit of the Abe and Ann story, then something of the influence on the young Lincoln of the New Salem countryside, then sidling off to an analysis of Lincoln's pioneer forebears. "Never forget," he interrupted himself at one point when he felt he had wandered too far afield, "that Lincoln gazed on these scenes, which aided to educate him. Never forget this for one moment.... Remember it was amid these scenes he loved and despaired, and—but I must pass on."

The first extended reference to Ann herself came near the start of the lecture, when Herndon, with disappointing brevity, described her as "a beautiful girl of New Salem ... an amiable and lovely girl of nineteen ... gifted with a good mind." No less than three young men of the village, he said, had been in love with her at the same time. These were the impecunious, twenty-five year old Lincoln and two well-off village businessmen, neither of whom he named. Rapidly, he went on to sketch an affecting yet somewhat mystifying situation:

> Circumstances, fate, Providence, the iron chain of sweeping events, so willed it that this young lady was engaged to Mr. Lincoln and Mr. —— at one and the same time. No earthly blame can be attached to the girl, and none to the men in their fidelity and honor to her. It all so happened, or was decided by fate. It shall, in truth, be explained hereafter to the satisfaction of all. It is a sad, thrilling story. The young girl saw her condition. Her word of promise was out to two men at the same time, both of whom she loved, dearly loved. The consciousness of this, and the con-flict of duties, love's promises, and womanly engagements, made her think, grow sad, become restless and nervous. She suffered, pined, ate not, and slept not. Time and struggle, as supposed and believed by many, caused her to have a raging fever, of which she died on the 25th day of August, A.D. 1835. She died on a farm seven miles north, bearing a little west of New Salem, and now lies buried in the Concord graveyard.

He had already paid a visit to Ann's grave, he said. Guided by a local resident, on the day before his visit to New Salem he had gone to the Concord burial ground four miles above Petersburg to search for the thirty-year-old site. The Concord cemetery was small, covering no more than an acre on the west bank of Berry's Creek, and he had soon located and verified Ann's grave. "The village of the dead is a sad, solemn place," he told his audience, "and when out in the country, especially so. Its very presence imposes truth on the mind of the living writer."

Having given his audience just enough to tease, Herndon switched direction and conjured up a life-size portrait of New Salem itself, along with some detail of Lincoln's life there. After speaking for some minutes, he again altered direction and went, not back to Ann, but into another long digression in which he analyzed the character of the American pioneer (a topic compelling enough in itself, it should be said, and very ably handled by Herndon). It was only as the evening drew to a close that he settled once more, still in his peculiarly abrupt fashion, on his principal theme. "Abraham Lincoln loved Miss Ann Rutledge with all his soul, mind, and strength," he suddenly announced, quickly adding that "she loved him as dearly." In this final half hour, he offered what amounted to a quick sketch of the love affair, and for the first time there was mention of *"The Poem."* Despite its length, for its full effect this part of the lecture must be given in the exact words Herndon used that night:

They seemed made in heaven for each other, though opposite in many things. As before remarked, she was accidentally, innocently, and honestly engaged to A. Lincoln and Mr. —— at one and the same time. It is said and thought that the young lady was conditionally promised to Mr. Lincoln, to be consumated upon her release from her first engagement to Mr. ——. The primary causes, facts and conditions which led to this complication shall be related to you at another time and place. There is no dishonor in it to any of the three. In her conflicts of honor, duty, love, promises, and womanly engagements, she was taken sick. She struggled, regretted, grieved, became nervous. She ate not, slept not, was taken sick of brain fever, became emaciated, and was fast sinking in the grave. Lincoln wished to see her. She silently prayed to see him. The friends of both parties at first refused the wish and prayer of both, still the wishes and prayers of both prevailed.

Mr. Lincoln did go to see her about the 10th day of August, A.D. 1835. The meeting was quite as much as either could bear, and more than Lincoln, with all his coolness and philosophy, could endure. The voice, the face, the features of her, the love, sympathy and interview fastened themselves on his heart and soul forever. Heaven only knows what was said by the two. God only knows what was thought. Dr. Jason Duncan of New Salem, about September 1833, had shown and placed in Mr. Lincoln's hands, the poem called in short "Immortality," or properly "Oh, Why should the spirit of mortal be proud?"

Leaving the subject of the poem dangling, Herndon shifted his attention to the grieving lover. What he said now, as everyone in the audience promptly realized, carried implications that went well beyond the concerns of the moment. To appreciate the full impact of this passage, it should be recalled that Lincoln's wife, then living in Chicago, was still in deep mourning, and that there existed many rumors of the Lincolns' marital strife, caused largely, as it was believed, by Mary Lincoln's difficult personality. Reminding his hearers that the Concord cemetery lay less than thirty miles from where they were sitting, Herndon now proceeded to paint an arresting portrait of the bereaved lover's state of mind:

> Mr. Lincoln has stated that his heart, sad and broken, was buried there. He said in addition to the same friend "I cannot endure the thought that the sleet and storm, frost and snow of heaven should beat on her grave." He *never* addressed another woman, in my opinion, "yours affectionately;" and generally and characteristically abstained from the use of the word "love." That word cannot be found more than a half dozen times, if that often, in all his letters and speeches, since that time. I have seen some of his letters to other ladies, but he never says "love." He never ended his letters with "yours affectionately," but signed his name, "your friend, A. Lincoln."

In other, plainer words, the man who had occupied the White House during the late fratricidal war had never really loved the woman he married and who had borne him four sons. Further, and far more troubling, he had been throughout his adult life in some sense, and to some degree, an emotional cripple. But a worse shock was to follow. Rushing on, Herndon informed his hearers that their late president, bowed down by his excessive grief over Ann's death, had teetered on the verge of actual insanity:

> He sorrowed and grieved, rambled over the hills and through the forests, day and night. He suffered and bore it for a while like a great man—a philosopher. He slept not, he ate not, joyed not. This he did until his body became emaciated and weak, and gave

way. His mind wandered from its throne. In his imagination, he muttered words to her he loved. His mind, his reason, somewhat dethroned, walked out of itself along the uncolumned air, and kissed and embraced the shadows and illusions of the heated brain. Love, future happiness, death, sorrow, grief, and pure and perfect despair, the want of sleep, the want of food, a cracked and aching heart, over and intense thought, soon worked a partial wreck of body and mind. It has been said that Mr. Lincoln became and was totally insane at that time and place.

Having drawn this unsparing picture of a sadly demented Lincoln, Herndon felt it prudent to draw back somewhat from so extreme a vision. The claim of total insanity, he went on, "is not exactly truth. The dethronement of his reason was only partial, and could alone be detected by his closest friends, and sharpest observers." Promptly, however, he ignored his own mild caveat and proceeded to enforce the idea of actual insanity, even if temporary. Trying to make graphic Lincoln's disturbed mental state, he bizarrely entered on a protracted soliloquy, imagined as having been spoken by the fuddled Lincoln as he wandered in solitude through the New Salem hills. In the circumstances it was a thoroughly peculiar indulgence (of Shakespearean derivation, and largely by way of the melancholy Hamlet) though it may well, sounding better than it now reads, have had the desired effect that night. In the curious passage, there is only the most fleeting mention of the cause of the sorrow, but it is couched in phrases that probably left a powerful impression on the rapt audience:

Ah! dead and gone from me thou sweet one; and shall this aching, crushed heart of mine never die and feel the pangs of nature never more. . . . Ah! dead and gone, thou sweet one, dead and buried forever, forevermore in the grave. . . . I love her and shall marry her on tomorrow's eve. So soul be content, and endless joy shall come. Heart of mine be still, for remember sweet tomorrow eve. . . . What! did I dream? Think, what did I say? It cannot be. She's dead and gone—gone forever. Fare thee well, sweet girl! We'll meet again.

All New Salem became aware of young Lincoln's dangerous mental condition, claimed Herndon, and all tried generously to help him overcome his grief, especially the women. But no sympathy, no cajolery, had any effect as Lincoln morosely refused "to quit the places and scenes of his sorrow." At last an old friend, Bowling Green, along with others, persuaded him to go to the Green house about a mile out of New Salem, where he could rest in private under the care of Green's wife, Nancy:

> In the space of a week or ten days, by Bowling's humor, generosity, and hospitality, his care and kindness, aided by the womanly sympathy, gentleness and tenderness of his wife, Lincoln soon rose up, a man once more. He was visited daily by men, women, boys and girls, whose conversation, stories, jokes, witticisms, fun and sport, soon roused up the man, thus enabling him to momentarily throw off sorrow, sadness, grief, pain and anxiety. They walked over the hills with him, danced for him, read for him, laughed for him, and amused him in a thousand ways. He evidently enjoyed all, as man scarcely ever enjoyed two weeks before, nor since. He got well and bade adieu for a short season to Bowling's kind roof and generous hospitality. Mrs. Bowling Green still lives, God bless her! and survives her own husband, and their ward and guest. Mr. Lincoln went back to New Salem, as thought, a changed, a radically changed man.

With only a few minutes of his time remaining, Herndon at last got back to the poem. That the living Lincoln, a regular reader of poetry, had shown exceptional fondness for some verses entitled *Mortality* was one of those small facts widely known to the public of his day. Many people, in fact, believed that Lincoln himself had written the poem, an error possible because the true author, an obscure young Scotsman by the name of William Knox, was then deceased. But in returning to the poem Herndon fudged on his promise made at the start to give its "history" in connection with Abe and Ann. The little information he did provide turned out to be only an excuse for declaiming the poem.

When the recovered Lincoln returned to the familiar scenes of New Salem, Herndon explained, he soon took up his favorite poem again, and read and re-read it. "He saw new beauties in it. He seized it and it seized him—a mutual seizure and arrest. He learned it by heart, committed it to memory, and repeated it over and over to his friends." Wisely, Herndon did not hold forth on the poem's attraction for

Lincoln but simply brought his lecture to a conclusion by reciting all fourteen quatrains, allowing the verses to suggest their own relevance. Here, half of the fourteen stanzas will suffice, with particular attention to the third:

> Oh, why should the spirit of mortal be proud?
> Like a swift-flying meteor, a fast-fleeting cloud,
> A flash of the lightning, a break of the wave,
> He passeth from life to his rest in the grave.
>
> The leaves of the oak and the willow shall fade,
> Be scattered around and together be laid;
> And the young and the old, and the low and the high,
> Shall moulder to dust and together shall lie.
>
> The maid on whose cheek, on whose brow, in whose eye
> Shone beauty and pleasure, her triumphs are by;
> And the memory of those who loved her and praised,
> Are alike from the minds of the living erased.
>
> So the multitude goes, like the flower or the weed,
> That withers away to let others succeed;
> So the multitude comes, even those we behold,
> To repeat every tale that has often been told.
>
> The thoughts we are thinking our fathers would think;
> From the death we are shrinking our fathers would shrink;
> To the life we are clinging they also would cling—
> But it speeds from us all like a bird on the wing.
>
> Yea, hope and despondency, pleasure and pain,
> Are mingled together in sunshine and rain;
> And the smile and the tear, the song and the dirge,
> Still follow each other like surge upon surge.
>
> 'Tis the wink of an eye, 'tis the draught of a breath,
> From the blossom of health to the paleness of death,
> From the gilded saloon to the bier and the shroud—
> Oh, why should the spirit of mortal be proud?

Before delivering the lecture, Herndon had arranged for its printing as a broadside, and promptly on the morning of November 17 gossiping Springfield residents found it available on newsstands and at bookstores. Copyright had been taken out in Herndon's name, but he had no intention of restricting his lecture's circulation by encumbering the reprint rights. "Newspapers as such," he encouraged in a footnote, "may use the lecture as they please," and scarcely one of the leading and even secondary papers around the country failed to take advantage of the invitation. Naturally, all concentrated—some favorably, many in fervent disapproval—on the love story and its disturbing picture of a loveless and sadly distraught Lincoln. Most agreed that, even if everything Herndon said were true, the story should not have been made public while memories of the martyred president were still so painful. Others thought that if he was going to make the story public at all, then he should have supplied his proofs, should have laid out the evidence that he claimed lay so tantalizing in the bureau drawers at his home.

An example of the soberer and more objective reaction, by the public and in print, was the comment that accompanied a partial reprint of the lecture in the *New York Times*. The paper thanked Herndon for throwing needed light on the president's character, specifically on those "melancholy and abstracted moods" observed by so many of Lincoln's friends, "and which no one hitherto has attempted to explain."

2

The Legend Grows

WHO WAS the mystery man in the case, readers wanted to know, that unnamed gentleman whose engagement to Ann had preceded Lincoln's? If Ann had really been the noble girl described, how in the first place had that strange double promise of hers arisen? No hint of an answer to these matters had been breathed in the lecture. But Herndon, who was at heart and in certain moods a somewhat naive and trusting soul, in talking casually with certain interested parties who came to visit him from the East, had not been quite guarded enough. Through the eyes of two of these visitors the public was now offered further curious information to ponder.

One, a Boston journalist named Caroline Dall, had managed to talk with Herndon even before the lecture. Impressed by the woman's New England background, carried away by her ardently expressed interest in all connected with Lincoln and the pioneer days, he had told her more of the Ann Rutledge story than he intended. During a day spent at his home he had even allowed her to read some of the pertinent documents, at this point a privilege shown to no one except his wife. One of the first copies of the printed broadside of the lecture had also gone to Mrs. Dall, and as a result within three weeks of Herndon's lecture she was in print in the *Boston Advertiser* with new facts and extended commentary. Cast as a letter to the editor, her lengthy article was prominently treated by the Boston paper and by the many other papers that reprinted it, usually on the front page.

If Ann Rutledge had lived, wrote Mrs. Dall, and she and Lincoln had married, then Lincoln "would never have sought political life." As all his Springfield friends vouched, his tastes had been wholly domestic. Further, his having borne the terrible sorrow of Ann's death in silence for so long explained "many significant facts" about him, not least his known tendency for years afterward to be "reckless, despairing, atheistic." The dual engagement, with its conflicts of honor, love, and duty, was seen as sufficient in itself to bring on the girl's death. Delicate-natured Ann had been

> betrothed, before Mr. Lincoln ever saw her, to a Scotch merchant. In those days Illinois was as far from New York as Kamchatka now is. They were soon to be married, when the Scotchman went for business purposes to that city. For months nothing was heard of him; it was supposed that he was dead or had wickedly deserted Ann. The truth was that he lay ill of delirious fever at a small wayside inn. In this state of things, while Ann's mind was tortured by suspense and disappointment, Mr. Lincoln went to her father's house to board. In time a sort of provisional engagement ensued. There were circumstances in both lives which depressed and pained; they learned to hold each other very dear. Upon this state of things broke the rumor of the recovered Scotchman's return. The delicate nature of the woman broke under it. Betrothed to two—both of whom she loved—she had no choice but to die.

The Scotsman's name was not divulged by Mrs. Dall, if she even knew it, though she did state that the man was still alive, and still living in the New Salem vicinity. Before delivering his lecture, she said, Herndon had shown the manuscript to the Scotsman, who had read and approved "every line" of it.

Another visitor to Herndon in Springfield had been the then well-known correspondent of the *New York Tribune,* George Townsend. He too had come away with voluminous notes of an interview, which he proceeded to turn into an article, one of substantial length, mostly concerning Ann. With some minor differences, and one large one, his version of the love story paralleled that of Mrs. Dall, though here the cause of the girl's death is made slightly more specific, if hardly less curious. When the return of the still nameless Scotsman was delayed by his sudden illness, rumor started that he had run away to avoid marrying his lady; and, waiting some time in vain to hear from him, she received anew the attentions of Mr. Lincoln. About the time when they passed from courtesy to tenderness, and marriage between them was more than hinted at, the sick man returned like a ghost, gauged the condition of affairs, and upbraided the lady with fickleness. She had a delicate sense of honor, and felt keenly the shame of having seemed to trifle with two gentlemen at once; this preyed upon her mind till her body, not very strong, suffered by sympathy, and Mr. Herndon has oral and written testimony that the girl died out of regret at the equivocal position she had unwittingly assumed. The names of all the parties he has given me but I do not care to print them.

Townsend was the only writer in the history of the legend to suggest that McNamar had returned, like a ghost or otherwise, to New Salem while Ann still lived, so it may be said immediately that such was not the case. The hurrying journalist in Springfield, taking notes as the accommodating Herndon rambled on, simply got it wrong. That McNamar "upbraided the lady" was Townsend's own fictional touch, obviously added to heighten the drama—it could not have come from Herndon. Ann's brother Robert, reading a partial reprint of the Townsend story in the *St. Louis Democrat*—entitled "Lincoln's Early Love"—wrote disgustedly to Herndon that it showed a "reckless disregard" of facts and inflicted on both his sister and Lincoln a "great injustice." He was sure, Robert added, that the mistakes were the fault not of Herndon but the journalist.

Townsend also went a step further in another direction, making brutally explicit the veiled hints of both Herndon and Mrs. Dall concerning the Lincolns' marriage. As the stark words are perused on this page it should be remembered that on their original appearance they were certainly read by the deeply grieving Mary Lincoln, marking perhaps the first time she had seen such charges in print:

On the dead woman's grave Mr. Lincoln promised himself never to marry. This vow he kept very long. His marriage was in every respect advantageous to him. It whetted his ambition, did not nurse too much a penchant for home indolence that he had, and taught him particularly that there was something called society, which observed one's boots as well as his principles. He was always a loyal and reverent husband, a gentle but not positive father, and his wife saw the presidency for him before the thought of it troubled him.

With all possibility of true love obliterated by his profound sorrow at Ann's death, Townsend is saying, Lincoln's marriage had been one of convenience. The by then cold and calculating young lawyer had taken Mary as his bride solely out of a wish to link himself with the aristocratic Todds. His resulting troubled home life, broadly implied by Townsend's careful phrasing, had been the means of sending him out into the world, instead of permitting him to indulge his "indolence." And it was not Lincoln who had initially sought high political success but his hard, ambitious—"unloved" is implied—wife.

A month or so after the Townsend article went the rounds of the newspapers—it was also quickly made into a pamphlet—Mrs. Dall was back with a second effort of her own. An expanded version of her *Advertiser* letter now showed up as a long article, entitled "Pioneering," in the *Atlantic Monthly*. In the Rutledge portion, Ann again dies for no other reason than that she found herself engaged to two men and therefore "had no choice." Lincoln's mental balance again gives way under the shock of his fiancée's death, and again "all the resources of the neighborhood were exhausted to restore him to himself." Once more Lincoln is heard to murmur that his heart "lies buried in the grave of that girl," and again the Scotsman is permitted to remain unidentified.

New in the article, however, and of some significance, was a remark directly attributed to Herndon stating the reason of Lincoln's final commitment to the business of politics. "The love and death of this girl," Herndon is quoted as saying, "shattered Lincoln's purposes and tendencies. He threw off his infinite sorrow only by leaping wildly into the political arena." How that claim might be reconciled with the view that Lincoln's leap into politics was to escape a difficult wife and a troubled home was not addressed.

The simple romance that had flourished so briefly and ended so sadly in the log huts of a long-vanished midwestern town now bid fair to take on major historical importance.

The Rutledge tavern as it appears today in the restored village of New Salem. *Below:* Interior of the restored tavern suggesting how the public kitchen–dining room may have looked in Lincoln's day. *(Historic Sites Division, Illinois Historic Preservation Agency)*

Mary Ann Rutledge (née Miller), mother of Ann, about 1870 when she was in her eighties. Six of her ten children are shown below and on the following pages. *(Illinois State Historical Library)*

Robert Rutledge, about 1864, when he served as a provost marshal in the Union Army.

Jean (Jane) Rutledge, about 1860. Eldest of the Rutledge girls, she died before Herndon could speak with her.

Nancy Rutledge (Mrs. Prewitt), about 1860. She remembered young Abe's visits to her home.

John Rutledge, about
1855. Of young Abe, his
comrade-in-arms, he said,
"a better man never
lived."

William Blackburn Rutledge.
Eight years old at his sister's
death, he lived to 1917.

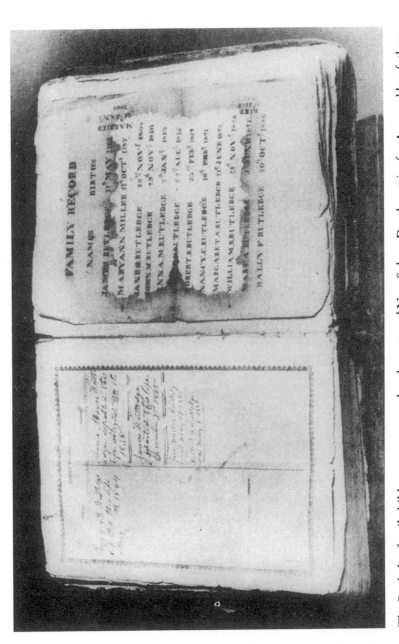

The Rutledge family bible, now preserved at the restored New Salem. Death entries for Ann and her father—they died four months apart—are in the upper right corner of the left-hand page.

Sarah (Sally) Rutledge, about 1880. Last of the New Salem Rutledges, she lived past the First World War. *(Illinois State Historical Library)*

James McGrady Rutledge, favorite cousin and confidant of Ann, about 1885. He said Ann and Abe were engaged. *(Illinois State Historical Library)*

The grave of Ann Rutledge in Oakland Cemetery, Petersburg, Illinois, her second resting place. Inscribed on the square granite headstone are the well-known verses of Edgar Lee Masters. *(Illinois State Historical Library)*

William Herndon, Lincoln's law partner, about 1885. Most of what is known of the Ann Rutledge legend, and much else about the young Lincoln, was discovered through his sole effort. *(Illinois State Historical Library)*

One of the two known documentary references to the living Ann Rutledge is this postscript in a letter written by her brother to his father, dated a month before Ann's death. The other is a note in *Kirkham's Grammar* (see the appendix). *(Illinois College, Jacksonville)*

Some ten years after the death of Ann Rutledge the thirty-seven-year-old Lincoln posed for this daguerreotype in Springfield. Husband, father of four, successful lawyer and congressman, his tight-fitting clothes and slick haircomb reflect the fashions of the day, concessions he would later ignore. *(Library of Congress)*

By the summer of 1869 William Herndon had become a dejected and disappointed man. Circumstances, seemingly permanent, had brought a halt to all his hopes of writing the first detailed and candid biography of Abraham Lincoln, a task he had long envisioned as "my duty . . . my religion."

By now beyond Herndon's control were such problems as the need to make up for his serious neglect of his law practice while engaged in his Lincoln research, especially critical in the financial depression of the late sixties. Also getting out of control was an old failing of his, an inclination under stress to drink too much (he may have been an alcoholic, as is charged, but if so it should also be recorded that he eventually conquered the fault). But more fatal than either of these shortcomings to the proposed work was his lack of all talent for book writing. Possessor of some native skill in description, wielder of a nervously colorful prose style, he could express himself effectively only in bursts and had not the least notion how to organize his materials into a coherent narrative.

The deciding factor in his surrender, however, was certainly his worsening financial condition. In the fall of 1869, after lengthy negotiations, Herndon sold his entire Lincoln research to another hopeful Lincoln biographer—voluminous notes of interviews, extensive correspondence, and many memoranda of his own observations, the whole making what he called his "Lincoln Record," bound in three thick leather volumes. For it he was to receive four thousand dollars, a fairly large sum then, and the bill of sale shows that he gave up all rights to the unique material, specifying that the purchaser was now able to use it "as he wishes." As it turned out, the new biography, produced with the aid of a ghostwriter by Lincoln's friend Ward Lamon, was in substance—though lacking his verbal flare—very close to the book Herndon himself might have written.

Urged by Lamon to provide additional information on Lincoln out of his personal knowledge and experience, Herndon responded willingly, sending a stream of vivid if woefully rambling letters, copies of all his lectures, and additional lengthy essays on almost every aspect of Lincoln's career, including the Rutledge romance. Gratefully received by Lamon, much of this added matter was used in the finished book, being duly credited to Herndon. In June 1872 a large volume of 582 crowded pages was published, and at last the public had what purported to be a full and accurate account of Abe and Ann's love story. Occupying a chapter of its own, it fixed the basic legend almost in its final form, much as it would be known ever after.

What follows is a shortened version of the Lamon chapter, edited to sharpen and clarify the lumbering old style. It is quoted here in place of the usual running paraphrase as a more faithful way of presenting this pivotal stage of the developing story. (Of course, none of the deletions alter the sense of what Lamon wrote originally.)

A statement that ends the Lamon chapter more properly belongs at its opening, so is here moved forward. As Lamon explained, the whole substance of his Rutledge revelations was derived from Herndon himself, mainly by way of the lecture, which was delivered and circulated "without contradiction" from any quarter, including old residents of New Salem and the Rutledge family. To this original exposition, added Lamon, there had been joined an unidentified "mass of additional evidence," most of it again deriving from Herndon. Included was the name of Ann's first love.

At the chapter's opening the reader has already been introduced to James Rutledge, Ann's father, as one of the two founders of the village of New Salem. An intrepid Kentuckian with roots in South Carolina and possible family ties to a signer of the Declaration of Independence, the elder Rutledge gave the little village its initial feeling of solidity when he erected first the mill and then the tavern:

> Mr. Rutledge kept the tavern on the main street of New Salem, just opposite Lincoln's grocery. There Mr. Lincoln came to board late in 1832 or early in 1833. The family consisted of father, mother, and nine children. Ann, the third child, was born on the 7th of January 1813, so was about nineteen when Lincoln came to live at the house.
>
> When Ann had just turned seventeen and was still at school, there came to New Salem a gentleman of singular enterprise. He took boarding with Mr. Rutledge's friend and partner, John Cameron, and gave out his name as John McNeil. He had no other capital than good sense and a plucky spirit, but somehow fortune smiled on all his endeavors. As early as the latter part of 1832 he found himself a prosperous man, owning a snug farm seven miles north of New Salem, and a half-interest in the largest store of the place. This latter property his partner, Samuel Hill, bought from him, for McNeil had announced his intention of

being absent for a brief period, and his purpose was such that he might need all his available capital.

In the meantime, the partners, Hill and McNeil, had both fallen in love with Ann Rutledge, and both courted her. But the contest had long since been decided in favor of McNeil, and Ann loved him with all her susceptible heart. When the time drew near for McNeil to depart he confided to Ann a strange story, and in the eyes of a person less fond, a startling story. His name was not John McNeil at all, but John McNamar.* His family was a respectable one in the state of New York; but a few years earlier his father had failed in business and there was great distress at home. John had then conceived the romantic plan of running away, and in the far west making a fortune with which to retrieve the family disaster. He fled, changed his name to avoid pursuit, found his way to New Salem, and—she knew the rest.

He was now able to perform the act of filial piety he had set out to accomplish. He would return at once to the relief of his parents in New York State, and would bring them back with him to his new home in Illinois. He would return as speedily as the journey could be made. Ann believed this tale, because she loved the man that told it.

On an antiquated steed, McNamar jogged through the long journey from New Salem to New York. He arrived there after many delays only to find that his father, broken and dispirited, was fast sinking into the grave. After all his efforts he was too late; his father could never enjoy the prosperity his long-absent son had brought him. McNamar wrote Ann that there was sickness in the family and he could not return at the time appointed. Then there were other and still other postponements, delayed departures all due to circumstance, until years had rolled away and Ann's heart had grown sick with hope deferred.

Ann never quite gave McNamar up, but continued to expect him until death terminated her melancholy watch. His inexplicable delay, however, the infrequency of his letters, and their unsatisfactory character—these and something else had broken

---

*Pronunciation of the name is uncertain. In Illinois today it is given as Mac-*nay*-mer or Mac-*nam*-mer. But since it is a contraction of the actual family name, McNamara, it is also pronounced as *Mac*-nuh-*mar*.

her attachment for McNamar, and toward the last she waited for him only to ask a release from her engagement, to say that now she preferred another. Without McNamar's formal renunciation of his claim on her, however, she did not like to marry. In obedience to this refinement of honor she postponed her union with this second lover until August 25, 1835 when, as many persons believe, she died of a broken heart.

Lamon's clumsy transition from McNamar to an unnamed "second lover," whom Ann came to prefer just before dying, is followed by an equally inept leap backward. He now takes up the period before Ann's death—apparently the latter part of 1833—when the Rutledge family had sold the tavern in New Salem and moved to a farm some six miles north, in the hamlet of Sandridge. Here Lincoln comes on stage already established as an active suitor of the girl:

Lincoln's friend, James Short, was in some way related to the Rutledges, and for a while Lincoln visited Ann two or three times a week at his house. According to him, "Miss Rutledge was a good-looking, smart, lively girl, a good housekeeper, with a moderate education, and without any of the so-called accomplishments." Nult Green is even more enthusiastic: "Her intellect was quick, sharp, deep, and philosophic, as well as brilliant.... She was beloved by everybody, so sweet and angelic was she. She was a woman worthy of Lincoln's love."* McNamar, her unfortunate lover, says, "Miss Ann was a gentle, amiable maiden, without any of the airs of your city belles, but winsome and comely withal; a blond in complexion, with golden hair, cherry-red lips, and a bonny blue eye."

Even the women of the neighborhood united to praise this beautiful but unhappy girl. Mrs. Hardin Bale knew her well and says that she had "auburn hair, blue eyes, fair complexion; was a slim, pretty, kind, tender, good-hearted woman; in height about five feet three inches, and weighed about a hundred and twenty pounds. She was beloved by all who knew her. She died as it were of grief."

When Mr. Lincoln first saw Ann she was probably the most

---

*The passage is actually from a letter of William G. Green (brother of Nult Green) to Herndon, May 30, 1865, to be quoted below.

refined woman with whom he had ever spoken, a modest, delicate creature, fascinating by contrast with the rude people surrounding her. It would be hard to trace the growth of this attachment at a time and place so distant; but that it actually grew and became an intense and mutual passion, the evidence before us is abundant.

Mr. Lincoln's visits were always welcome at the farm, half a mile from Short's, where the Rutledges finally abode. Ann's father was his devoted friend, and her mother he called affectionately Aunt Polly.

It is probable that the family looked upon McNamar's delay with more suspicion than Ann did herself. At all events, her relatives encouraged the suit which Lincoln began to press; and as McNamar's apparent neglect told gradually against him, she listened to Lincoln with augmenting interest until, in 1835, we find them formally betrothed.

That vague reference to 1835 is the only date employed by Lamon in connection with the progress or culmination of the romance. His failure even to attempt any chronological tracking, particularly with such items as McNamar's departure from New Salem, set the tone for all subsequent discussions, in fact up until quite recently. This early and continuing neglect of the time and sequence factors is one strong reason why the story for so long escaped any close scrutiny. Its seeming incoherence, apparently impenetrable, was its shield.

Ann now waited only for the return of McNamar to marry Lincoln. [Her brother] David urged her to marry immediately, without regard to anything but her own happiness; but she said she could not consent to it until McNamar released her from her pledge. However, as [time passed and] McNamar's appearance became more and more doubtful she took a different view, and thought she would become Abe's wife as soon as he found the means of a decent livelihood. "Ann told me once," says [her cousin] James, "that engagements made too far ahead sometimes failed; that one *had* failed (meaning her engagement to McNamar), and gave me to understand that, as soon as certain studies were completed, she and Lincoln would be married."

In the summer of 1835 Ann showed unmistakeable signs of failing health. Most of the neighborhood believed it was a result of the distressing attitude she felt bound to maintain between her two lovers. On the 25th of August 1835, she died of what the doctors chose to call "brain-fever." In a letter to Mr. Herndon her brother says, "You suggest that the probable cause of Ann's sickness was her conflicts, emotions, etc. As to this I cannot say. I however, have my own private convictions. The character of her sickness was brain-fever."

For many, perhaps most, readers at the time of the Lamon book's publication—seven years after Lincoln's death—it was the next section of the chapter, detailing aspects of Lincoln's terrible grief, that provided the most vital and absorbing revelations. To appreciate the grim appeal it exercised back then, today's reader need only picture something similar being said of such war presidents as Wilson, Roosevelt, or Truman: that a devastating youthful tragedy had made them "insane" for a period, in which they showed suicidal tendencies, and that they were "never precisely the same" afterward.

A few days before her death Lincoln was summoned to her bedside. What happened in that solemn conference was known only to him and the dying girl. But when he left her, and stopped at the house of his friend John Jones on his way home, Jones saw in his face and conduct signs of the most terrible distress. When Ann actually died his grief became frantic: he lost all self-control, even the consciousness of identity, and every friend he had in New Salem pronounced him insane, mad, crazy. "He was watched with especial vigilance," William Green tells us, "during storms, fogs, and damp gloomy weather for fear of an accident." At such times he raved piteously, declaring "I can never be reconciled to have the snow, rains, and storms beat upon her grave."

About three-quarters of a mile below New Salem, at the foot of the main bluff, stood the log house of Bowling Green. Thither the friends of Lincoln determined to transport him, partly for a change of scene, partly to keep him within constant reach of his noble friend. During this period of his darkened and wavering intellect, "accidents" were momentarily expected. When Green came for him, Lincoln was obstinate and it required the most artful practices of his friends to induce him to go. Lincoln remained down under the bluff for two or three weeks, the object of the

strictest surveillance. At the end of that time his mind seemed to
be restored, and it was thought safe to let him go back to his old
haunts.

But Mr. Lincoln was never precisely the same man again. At
the time of his release he was thin, haggard, and careworn—like
one risen from the verge of the grave. He had always been subject
to fits of great mental depression, but after this they were more
frequent and alarming. It was then that he began to repeat, with a
feeling that seemed to carry him to the fresh grave of Ann, the
lines beginning, "Oh! why should the spirit of mortal be proud?"
All who heard him knew that he selected these curiously empty,
yet wonderfully sad verses to celebrate a grief which lay continually on his heart, but to which he could not, with delicacy, alude
directly. He muttered them as he rambled through the woods,
walked by the roaring Sangamon, or slipped into the village at
nightfall after a visit to the Concord graveyard. They came unbidden to his lips, while the air of affliction in face and gesture, the
moving tones and touching modulations of his voice made it
evident that the recitation was meant to commemorate the mournful fate of Ann. Mr. Lincoln's adoption of the poem has saved it
from oblivion, and the poem is now his: the name of the obscure
author is forgotten, while his work is imperishably associated
with the memory of a great man.

Here Lamon mentions an incident from a small, highly popular
book of Lincoln reminiscences published in 1866, F. B. Carpenter's *Six
Months at the White House*. The anecdote recalls one night when the
brooding president in Carpenter's presence recited all fourteen verses of
the poem, Lincoln explaining to Carpenter that he had first read and
memorized it as a young man.

The Isaac Cogdal mentioned in the chapter's next section, was still
alive when Lamon's book came out, a widely known and much respected
lawyer practicing in the Springfield area. Lincoln's words, as reported,
must of course be seen as passing through a double refraction, Cogdal's
memory and Herndon's notetaking:

After Mr. Lincoln's election to the presidency, and before he left
for Washington, in Springfield one day he met an old friend, Isaac
Cogdal, who had know him intimately in New Salem. Lincoln

invited Cogdal to drop in at the state house that evening to talk over old times, and he went. "When we lived in Salem," began Lincoln, "there were the Greens, Potters, Armstrongs, and Rutledges. These folks have got scattered all over the world—some are dead. Where are the Rutledges, Greens, etc.?"

"After we had talked of people and circumstances," said Cogdal, "in which he showed a wonderful memory, I then dared to ask him this question—Is it true that you fell in love with and courted Ann Rutledge?"

"It is true—true indeed. I did. I have loved the name of Rutledge to this day. I have kept my mind on their movements ever since, and love them dearly."

"Abe, is it true," still urged Cogdal, "that you ran a little wild about the matter?"

"I did really. I ran off the track. It was my first. I loved the woman dearly. She was a handsome girl; would have made a good, loving wife; was natural and quite intellectual, though not highly educated. I did honestly and truly love the girl, and think often, often, of her now."

Immediately after relating the Cogdal incident, Lamon abruptly records the return of McNamar to New Salem, "a few weeks after" Ann's death. When he encountered his old friend Lincoln soon afterward, he was "struck with the deplorable change in his appearance," but no further comments or observations are ventured. With him, McNamar had brought his mother and her family of several sons and daughters, and then, writes Lamon, "in December of that same year his mother died and was buried in the same graveyard with Ann." In reality, the woman lived another ten years, residing all the time with her son in the Sandridge area. (The confusion is with Ann's father, who died in December 1835.)

The Lamon chapter comes to an end with the downright claim that the story of Ann, Abe, and John McNamar, in all its details, "is as well proved as the fact of Mr. Lincoln's election to the presidency."

❧

At the time that Lamon revealed the name of Ann's first lover, McNamar was still very much alive, working his large farm near Sandridge, some miles north of New Salem. It is one of the more curious, and disappointing, aspects of the Rutledge story that no historian, no serious writer, at this time or later, bothered to approach him for further particulars. There was one fairly lengthy interview in 1874, in connection with the dedication of the Lincoln tomb in Springfield, but the hurried reporter brought out nothing new or significant about Ann. McNamar lived until 1879, marrying a second time when his first wife died and raising a large family, but leaving on record little beyond what he had earlier told Herndon. The few, not very informative letters in which he conveyed this information still exist. They will play their part in the unraveling further on.

After the Lamon book came the deluge, as the ill-fated romance of Abe and Ann entered the rising folklore about the dead president. In newspapers, magazine fiction, novels, plays, and poetry the story subtly grew in nuance and detail as it made its way out of history and into the popular imagination. Through it all, the aging Herndon stood unhappily on the sidelines, freely dispensing information about his old partner to any who asked, defending himself when necessary, if perhaps not with just the old vigor, and never quite letting go of his desire to give the public its first wholly candid and realistic portrait of the martyred leader. As he was well aware, however, he had neither the time nor the energy, certainly not the ability, to produce such a book, even if he could recover the rights to his "Lincoln Record." But then, as he entered his late sixties, with both desire and hope slipping fast away, the miracle happened. A young writer from Indiana named Jesse Weik, an avid student of Lincoln and the Civil War, who had corresponded with Herndon and had visited him in Springfield, eagerly consented to collaborate on a Lincoln biography.*

As it turned out, Weik brought Herndon exactly the type of assistance he needed, a skillful and patient writer-editor able to curb and guide the older man's exuberant waywardness. The wonderful result, published in 1889, few would have predicted. With all its faults of overemphasis and uncritical acceptance, the volume proved to be one of the most readable, informative, and valuable historical records ever produced in America, the classic *Herndon's Lincoln*.

During some four years the two men worked together, at all times in

---

*It is idle to ask why Herndon could not have enlisted similarly competent help years earlier. Perhaps he did not wish to share his task. Perhaps he could find no one willing to risk time, effort, and money as Weik did.

perfect harmony. From his home in Springfield, Herndon supplied Weik in Indiana with a confused mass of disjointed manuscript, including many dozens of freewheeling and repetitious letters, rambling essays, casual memoranda, and drafts of chapters. This flood of material Weik organized, edited, condensed, and rewrote into a publishable manuscript, in the process necessarily losing something of Herndon's reckless verve but doing no harm to the substance. The Ann Rutledge story received full attention, again being set off in a chapter by itself, of about the same length as Lamon's. Though Weik here, too, performed a good deal of smoothing, he was very careful to preserve his co-author's viewpoint and facts, introducing nothing beyond what Herndon had selected.

Calling the Ann Rutledge interlude emphatically "the saddest chapter in Mr. Lincoln's life," repeating his assertion that it was the source of permanent sorrow ("threw a melancholy shade over the remainder of his days"), Herndon now gave the twenty-five-year-old story the final touch. Showing how intimately he himself had been linked to the circumstances, he stated that he had known New Salem even before the arrival there of Lincoln, that as a young man he had often visited the Rutledge tavern and had known Ann personally (the brevity of the reference implies only a passing acquaintance). As a consequence, long before starting his Lincoln research, he had been familiar with "every one of the score or more witnesses whom I have at one time or another interviewed on this delicate subject." For someone with his background, however, and who claimed to have known Ann, the portrait he gave of her proved rather meager:

> She was a beautiful girl, and by her winning ways attached people to her so firmly that she soon became the most popular young lady in the village. She was quick of apprehension, industrious, and an excellent housekeeper. She had a moderate education, but was not cultured except by contrast with those around her. One of her strong points was her womanly skill. She was dexterous in the use of the needle.... At every "quilting" Ann was a necessary adjunct, and her nimble fingers drove the needle more swiftly than anyone's else. Lincoln used to escort her to and from these quilting-bees, and on one occasion even went into the house— where men were considered out of place—and sat by her side as she worked on the quilt.

The few significant items Herndon added to the Lamon treatment related to the question of Lincoln's grief and to McNamar's role. The Scotsman's use of the name McNeil, he said, was occasioned by his fear that if the family in New York had known where he was, "they would have settled down on him, and before he could have accumulated any property would have sunk him beyond recovery." The story's crux—McNamar's failure to return to New Salem in good time—was expanded on, though somewhat lamely, and was given in two parts:

In passing through Ohio he became ill with fever. For almost a month he was confined to his room, and a portion of the time was unconscious. As he approached a return to good health he grew nervous over the delay in his trip. He told no one around him his real name, destination, or business. He knew how his failure to write to New Salem would be construed, and the resulting irritation gave way to a feeling of desperation. In plainer language, he concluded it was "all up with him now."

Reaching his home in New York State—no more exact location was supplied—McNamar finds his father in declining health. Soon thereafter "the old gentleman gradually faded from the world," leaving McNamar to settle the bewildered family's affairs, with the added responsibility of seeing to its future:

His detention necessitated a letter to Ann, explaining the nature and cause of the delay. Other letters followed; but each succeeding one growing less ardent in tone, and more formal in phraseology than its predecessor, Ann began to lose faith. Had his love gradually died away like the morning wind? was a question she often asked herself. She had stood firm under fire before, but now her heart grew sick with hope deferred. At last the correspondence ceased altogether.

During McNamar's protracted absence, the long-smitten Lincoln was led to conclude that "the silken ties" between Ann and the absent Scotsman had been definitely broken. Only with that had the scrupulous Lincoln "ventured to step in himself." The perplexed Ann, having known Lincoln well for three years or more, and under the favorable urging of all her family, at length accepted his proposal, "provided he gave her time to write to McNamar and obtain his release from her pledge." The letter was sent and the long weeks passed, but no answer ever came. No reason is given for McNamar's continued silence, but at last Ann agreed to go ahead with plans for her marriage to Lincoln:

> Now that they were engaged he told her what she already knew, that he was poverty itself. She must grant him time to gather up funds to live on until he had completed his law studies. . . . to this the thoughtful Ann consented. To one of her brothers she said, "As soon as his studies are completed we are to be married."

Ann's fatal illness is again set down as the simple result of an emotional "conflict," which receives no further description. Not at all clear, however, is the exact shape or nature of her difficulty, whether anguished indecision between the love of two men or a mortal fear that she might have unwittingly compromised herself in a matter of honor:

> But the ghost of another love would often rise unbidden before her. Within her bosom raged the conflict which finally undermined her health. Late in the summer she took to her bed. A fever was burning in her head. Day by day she sank, until all hope was banished. During the latter days of her sickness, her physician had forbidden visitors to enter her room, prescribing absolute quiet. But her brother relates that she kept inquiring for Lincoln so continuously, at times demanding to see him, that the family at last sent for him. On his arrival at her bedside the door was closed and he was left alone with her. What was said, what vows and revelations were made during this sad interview, were known only to him and the dying girl. A few days afterward she became unconscious and remained so until her death.

The immediate, crushing effect of Ann's death on Lincoln's calm and stoical makeup, Herndon portrays starkly. In fits of deep depression the grieving lover, "woefully abstracted," wanders through the woods and beside the river. On these walks he is watched closely by his worried neighbors who feared that he would "take his own life." Resting finally in seclusion at the home of Bowling Green, he is gradually brought "back to reason, or at least of a realization of his true condition." This timely aid given him by his friends he was never to forget. When Bowling Green himself died six years later, Lincoln was asked to speak at the funeral. He did so but had to break off his eulogy when he could not hold back the tears.

No doubt feeling that by then the old poem *Mortality* had become well enough known, Herndon omits quoting it. But he does not neglect to mention that Lincoln had committed it to memory and would often willingly recite all fifty-six lines. The Isaac Cogdal incident he also repeats, at shorter length, adding that the story was told him personally by Cogdal, a man he had long known as an original New Salemite. As the Rutledge chapter ends, the permanent and pervading nature of Lincoln's grief is not only again made explicit but is made to point ominously into the distant future: "There is no question that from this time forward Mr. Lincoln's spells of melancholy became more intense than ever."

ॐ

At a fragile seventy-two years of age, with Scribner's in New York about to publish a third edition of his Lincoln biography, in March 1891 the weary but satisfied William Herndon died. Unfortunately, he had lived just long enough to hear of a last, thoroughly distasteful act in connection with the Ann Rutledge story. It was an incident, ironically, that may well have been prompted by the renewed notoriety given the old romance by means of Herndon's own book.

On the morning of May 15, 1890, an open flatbed wagon carrying four men and a boy drew up to the old Concord burying ground, some four miles north of Petersburg. With two of the men carrying shovels, the party entered the small, bush-strewn, overgrown cemetery. After searching among the scatter of weathered headstones, they stopped before one that announced the grave of Ann's brother David. While the diggers waited, the other two men talked. Older of the two was James McGrady Rutledge, aged seventy-six, favorite cousin of Ann and one of the few still alive who had attended her funeral in 1835 (it was a simple service, he would recall, and the sermon was preached by the Rev. John Camron, cofounder with Ann's father of New Salem). The other man was Samuel Montgomery of Petersburg, undertaker, furniture dealer, and secretary of Petersburg's own large burial ground, Oakland Cemetery.

For some minutes the two men held a murmured conference, the elderly Rutledge showing a mixture of reluctance and bewilderment. Alternately and uncertainly, he pointed a trembling finger at the tangle of grass that lay on either side of David's plot. When at last he mumbled that he could not be sure on which side lay his cousin, Montgomery turned to the two diggers and said they would have to excavate on both sides.

Soon exposed on the left was an old wooden coffin, but it proved to hold the remains of a child and it was covered up again. On the right side another coffin was found, its ends rotted. To the softened wood of the decaying lid a corroded nameplate still clung, and it identified the body as that of Ann Rutledge. Carefully the diggers removed the lid and soon the coffin's interior lay exposed, revealing a small mass of hair and a few bones. No clothing could be seen, only a small silver buckle and three buttons of pearl. Down into the grave Montgomery passed a large covered box, and to it the men transferred the whole contents of the coffin.

That night the box was stored at Montgomery's funeral parlor in Petersburg. Next morning it was taken up the hill to Oakland Cemetery, a distance of a half mile or so, where it was interred in the large, fenced plot awaiting it. Days later the announcement was made that the body of Lincoln's old sweetheart belonged to Petersburg. The sleepy old town, its citizens agreed, was now permanently on the map, ready to take its proper place in the booming Lincoln legend. At the same time, Montgomery assured the board of directors of Oakland Cemetery that they might now expect purchasers for the many unsold plots that had proved so hard to get rid of since the opening of the cemetery a decade before.

Blame for this sordid action does not attach wholly to Ann's aged and ailing cousin. The sole Rutledge relative then in the vicinity, when first approached by Montgomery for permission to move the body he had stoutly refused. Ann's sister Nancy, then living with her own family in Iowa, when approached had firmly supported the refusal: Ann's remains, she said, "should stay where those of her family were buried." But Montgomery, ambitious for himself and for his town, had pressured the old man into changing his mind, probably by convincing him that town sentiment was wildly in favor of the idea. He also explained that the grave would receive better care if accessible nearer town than it had been given over the decades at the disused Concord site. Whether the distant Nancy ever changed her mind is unknown.

Today, a century after the transfer, Ann's dust still rests in Oakland Cemetery. On the roads and highways nearby signs point the way to the large, squared-off boulder behind iron railings that serves as her headstone. One polished face of the boulder displays the well-known lines of Edgar Lee Masters in which the full-blown legend received its best known expression in brief:

> Out of me unworthy and unknown
> The vibrations of deathless music!
> "With malice toward none, with charity for all"
> Out of me forgiveness of millions toward millions,
> And the beneficent face of a nation
> Shining with justice and truth.
> I am Ann Rutledge who sleep beneath these weeds,
> Beloved of Abraham Lincoln,
> Wedded to him, not through union,
> But through separation.
> Bloom forever, O Republic,
> From the dust of my bosom!

Four miles to the north of Oakland Cemetery the old Concord Burial Ground also remains, still in the midst of widespreading fields, still the same obscure and inaccessible plot on a wooded mound that it was in Lincoln's day. Among its two hundred burials lie undisturbed the simple graves, marked by weathered stone slabs set in straggling rows, of many of the New Salem friends of Abe and Ann, men and women who had known at firsthand the truth about their romance.

3

Wavering Memories

"HE IS A dirty dog," wrote the stricken Mary Lincoln of William Herndon soon after hearing about and reading the original lecture. His life would not be worth living, she threatened, if he did not keep silent, "For I *have* friends, if his low soul thought that my great affliction left me without them." She had never in her life so much as heard the name of the dead girl, she insisted. Moreover, her husband had many times confessed to her that she herself was the only woman he had ever cared for: "Nor did his life or his joyous laugh lead one to suppose his heart was in any unfortunate woman's grave, but in the proper place with his loved wife and children." The Ann Rutledge story, she pronounced acidly, was a pathetic myth.

One friend of Mrs. Lincoln who did leap immediately to her defense, though without breathing threats of vengeance, was the Rev. James Smith, a Lincoln appointee as American consul in Scotland. Smith had known the Lincolns well as pastor of their church in Springfield and had often been a guest in their home. His defense of Mary Lincoln, based on his intimate personal knowledge of the family, took the form of a long letter to Herndon, with a copy sent to the *Dundee Advertiser* in hopes that the letter would be picked up by American papers. The wish was quickly gratified: on March 6, 1867, the *Chicago Tribune* carried it on the front page.

The burden of the clergyman's reply was the more or less expected one, already voiced in milder form at home. Herndon's "foul aspersions" had made Lincoln worse than a hypocrite, wrote Smith. As a young man he had wooed and won Mary when, "according to you, all he had to give in return was a dead heart buried in the grave of another woman, and he was in such a mental condition that he had to abstain from the use of the word love." Lincoln's children also stood condemned by Herndon's words, charged Smith, for they were now branded as "sons of a man who had never loved their mother." To the contrary, insisted the irate minister, during his seven years as the Lincolns' pastor he had gathered abundant proof that Lincoln had been "a most faithful, loving, and affectionate husband." Herndon was that execrable thing, "the false friend" who betrays.

There were many people besides Mary Lincoln who were glad to read the Smith rebuke in the *Tribune,* and to see it recopied in many other cities. The widow even had friends on the *Tribune* itself, it seems, for the next day the paper printed some follow-up comment, taking the unusual action of treating as a news story what amounted to an editorial. After some favorable comment on the Smith letter, the unsigned, front-page article launched into quite an emotional defense of Mrs. Lincoln, presenting her as the only love of her dead husband while insisting on the Lincolns' great domestic happiness. During the pair's twenty-three years of marriage, never by word or act did Lincoln give the merest hint "that his heart was absent, or was buried in some other woman's grave. . . . had he been the hypocrite and dissembler which modern romance would hold him up to the world as being, [no one] had the slightest cause to suspect it." On the great president's pitifully suffering wife Herndon had inflicted an unpardonable cruelty by giving currency to "this now exploded romance."

The Reverend Smith was only the first of many who would, in personal terms and without bothering much with evidence, roundly condemn Herndon's story. In the concluding decades of the nineteenth century, as the martyred president's star rose ever higher, there were not a few who voiced a firm belief that the Rutledge tale could not be accurate as Herndon had fashioned it. No doubt there had existed such an appealing village maiden. Probably young Lincoln had known her, possibly had felt something like love for her, may even have thought of marriage. But if so, it had amounted to no more than a passing episode, soon left behind, little different from the first, almost always ephemeral love of many a more ordinary man.

All the rest of the story, the part portraying Lincoln as weakly sinking into spells of lunacy at Ann's death, then bearing her memory as an open wound during his remaining years, was summarily dismissed as excessive, "too highly colored" by far. Evidence or no evidence, the great Civil War leader must be anticipated in his youth, and no more evenly balanced, solidly grounded personality, no saner man, had ever trod the burnished floors of the White House. His slightly mournful, wryly sad air, the melancholy that Herndon said "dripped from him as he walked," was seen as constitutional, an inheritance from his mother or from some more distant forebear. It could not in any sense be a legacy of a vague and fleeting sorrow of his youth, now long forgotten.

Among the few voices speaking out in support of the legend in these earlier years, there was one, quieter and less able to command attention, which unexpectedly bridged the long gap of time back to New Salem. In the summer of 1885, on the fiftieth anniversary of Ann's death, one of her sisters, Nancy Prewitt, then aged sixty-five, paid a nostalgic visit to the then all but vanished town. This unexpected reappearance of a Rutledge on the scene of the original drama led to a lengthy article in a Chicago paper, preserving an interview that for some reason has dropped out of sight in Lincoln studies.

Gone from the New Salem site was the log tavern whose remnants had been seen and described by Herndon twenty years before. But Mrs. Prewitt stood on "the very spot," as she called it, occupied by her father's old business, and she saw as well the remains of the old sawmill at the foot of the bluff, also built by her father. Having been fifteen years old at the time of her sister's death, her memories of Lincoln himself at new Salem were vivid: "I was only a child when he boarded at our house," she told a reporter, "and yet I remember just how he looked and talked, as well as if it were only last year." Asked if she considered Lincoln homely, she gave an answer of a type that has since become familiar:

> "Homely? Yes, I suppose he was, but I never thought of that then. I remember his tall, lank, ungainly figure, and his big ears and mouth, but when he talked one never thought of that. He was so good-natured and full of life and fun, and everybody loved him so well that they never thought of his looks. I can see him now, just as he looked, sitting by the big, old-fashioned fireplace, absorbed in a book or chatting merrily with Annie or one of my brothers. He always came and went just as one of the family.

Abe and Ann, she recalled, often sang together out of an old songbook hymns and the standard tunes of the day. "I have the very book he and Annie used," she assured the interviewer as she reached up and took from a shelf an old, green-backed volume called *The Missouri Harmony.**

Describing her sister, Mrs. Prewitt said that she was small, "with dark blue eyes, light brown hair, and a very fair complexion. Everyone said she was pretty." She readily confirmed the traditional view of the romance, insisting that "no one could have seen them together and not be convinced that they loved each other truly." As to the cause of Ann's death, she disagreed, recalling that the doctor had identified the disease as brain fever. While she could not vouch for the doctor's diagnosis, she was sure that Ann's death "was not caused by a broken heart or disappointed hopes."

Asked if she could supply a photograph of her sister, Mrs. Prewitt replied that there were none, and she explained that people "did not have pictures taken then as they do now." In this her memory served her better than most who have talked about possible photographs of the dead woman. In its earliest form photography was not given to the world until four years after Ann's passing.

These recollections of Ann's sister came at the right moment, for they helped feed that unquestioning popular acceptance of the legend that began to develop in earnest during the concluding decade of the nineteenth century—writers of all sorts not only accepted the Herndon version of the love story, they accepted all in addition that it seemed to imply or could be made to yield. The work done by Ida Tarbell, especially, first on assignment for *McClure's Magazine* and then subsequently in several well-received books, brought Ann's story its fullest expression (aside from avowedly fictional treatments), introducing it full-panoplied into the twentieth century. In ending her slim, heavily illustrated volume on Lincoln's early life, she takes leave of him at the very moment "when the tragic death of Ann Rutledge made all that he had attained, all that he had planned, seem fruitless and empty." When eventually he rallied, he was armed with new powers of "patience and insight" such as are derivable only from some "great sorrow." On the page just above those words appears a photograph of Ann's new grave in Oakland Cemetery.

---

*Herndon's comment on Lincoln's singing voice should not be passed over: "Could Lincoln sing? Can a pig whistle?" Others said about the same, less vividly.

ક*

When William Herndon died in 1891, his "Lincoln Record," containing all his original documents relating to New Salem and Ann Rutledge, was left in the hands of his collaborator, Jesse Weik. Thereafter for thirty years, and for reasons never explained, Weik held the record back, refusing all requests for its use even from reputable historians. It was no less a personage than former U.S. senator Albert Beveridge, then preparing a full-scale biography of Lincoln, who finally in the early twenties succeeded in prying the "Record" loose from Weik's stranglehold. Despite his lack of credentials as a professional historian, Beveridge had already gained respect for a work on Chief Justice John Marshall, so this first sustained and objective survey of the original evidence on the Rutledge legend was eagerly awaited.

While Beveridge was at work, William Barton, also an amateur but already in high repute as a Lincoln student, began study for a treatise to be called "The Women Lincoln Loved." The separate productions of these two men, earnest and capable students both, along with some work done simultaneously by a third nonprofessional, Carl Sandburg, will show better than anything else the confused and nearly unmanageable state the legend had reached by the twenties.

As Barton boldly announced, he was bent on producing the "most careful examination ever made" of the legend. It was a brave claim, even if it blandly ignored the fact that he had already been denied access to the primary documents in the case, the Herndon papers. Starting his research in fairly dramatic fashion, he journeyed in the summer of 1921 all the way to California to interview the last surviving member of the Rutledge family, Ann's youngest sister, Sarah, most often called Sally. A spry ninety-three, but having recently broken her hip, Sally Saunders was resting in a nursing home at Lompoc, near the coast some hundred miles above Los Angeles. Two of her sons, one a doctor, were caring for her, and they welcomed Barton's enthusiasm and his polite but probing questions as helping to lift their mother's spirits.

Though Barton was not the one who discovered Sally Saunders, her existence in California, where she had lived with her family for forty years, had been virtually unknown to the Lincoln fraternity. When the first stirrings of the plan to reconstruct New Salem surfaced in 1917, it was the elderly Mrs. Saunders herself, joyfully responding to the news, who established contact. Astonished to learn that one of the Rutledge sisters was still alive, the leaders of the reconstruction warmly welcomed her offer of several Lincoln relics (among them a pewter coffee pot used at the Rutledge tavern, a patchwork quilt containing pieces of Lincoln's clothing, a grammar textbook used in turn by him and Ann,[*] a leather riding saddle used by Ann, and a bible containing handwritten birth and death records of the Rutledge family). Barton, from the moment he heard of Sally Saunders's existence, was fiercely impatient to see and talk to her. Eventually, as he proudly recorded, he "crossed the continent" for that special purpose.

Propped on a couch under a blanket at the nursing home in Lompoc, Mrs. Saunders gave clear if sometimes hesitating replies to Barton's inquiries, "growing more animated as she talked." To allow the old lady a rest and to preserve her words exactly, every once in a while Barton went to another room to write down her replies, then returned and read her what he had written. At the interview's close she willingly put her signature to the manuscript in firm though slightly sprawling letters: Sarah Rutledge Saunders.

With unusual candor—considering how sore must have been the temptation to color things—she confessed that her personal knowledge of the love affair had come to her from her mother and her sisters. Born in New Salem at the Rutledge tavern in October 1829, almost two years before Lincoln's arrival, she had been too young herself to see or to understand much about her elder sister's romances. Lincoln himself she claimed to recall clearly, especially because of the many times she had been held on his lap: "I was the baby of the family and he was kind to the baby.... He was friendly with all of us girls, and while I knew that he cared especially for Ann, I have had to interpret what I saw and knew of their relations in the light of what my mother and my sister, Nan, told me." Lincoln, she volunteered at one point, liked singing very much, but "he could not sing very well," and she too specified the old songbook *The Missouri Harmony*.

Her personal memory of Ann was particularly poignant and loving, as well as fresh in her mind:

I can see sister Ann as she sat sewing from day to day, for she was the seamstress of the family, while the other girls, Nancy and

---

[*]This was the well-known volume of *Kirkham's Grammar*. However, it never reached New Salem, and today it is preserved at the Library of Congress. For further on this volume, see pp. 130–31 and the appendix.

Margaret, aided mother in the general housework and care of the
tavern. She taught me how to sew, and I remember her patience
with me, as well as her industry and kindness.... Ann was light
complexioned, her hair auburn. During her sickness her hair was
cut, and mother kept it for many years. After a time the moths
got into it and we had to destroy it. She had blue eyes and was
slender, and not very robust. All our memories and traditions of
her are of a sweet and beautiful character.

Curiously, Mrs. Saunders's view of John McNamar was decidedly a
negative one, and she was apparently the first to offer such an opinion.
Her father "never trusted him," she said, after hearing of the name
change, though the two had had business dealings. Her own dislike of
him seems to have centered on his actions after returning to New
Salem from his long stay in New York. As she recalled it, McNamar's
heartlessness was the cause of the Rutledges leaving Sangamon County:

I do not know by what means John McNamar acquired title to
father's farm. It has been said that he bought it after Ann's death
as a matter of sentiment. John McNamar was not a sentimental
man and he acquired the title before the death either of Ann or
my father. His alleged love for the memory of my dead sister
was not sufficient to shelter Ann's widowed mother in the home
which she had helped to build. That was why my mother had to
take her family of fatherless children and move to a new home in
Iowa. He turned Mother out. We had a hard time but at length
we made a home there.

At some point in the interview Barton suddenly struck gold. Casually,
the woman mentioned an old letter long cherished by her family,
describing it as one of the last mementos of her sister. Written by her
brother David, then away at school, to his father in New Salem, it
contained a brief aside to Ann. By next day the excited Barton was in
happy possession of the original letter—given to him as a loan—and
he immediately recognized its importance. At a glance he saw that it
lent strong support to one crucial aspect of the legend, the claim that
Ann, in order to fit herself to be a lawyer's wife, had meant to attend
school for a year at the Jacksonville Female Academy before marrying
Lincoln.

The body of the letter, dated July 27, 1835, and addressed to Mr. Rutledge, talks of David's personal plans. There are two brief postscripts, one to be passed on to a friend and one for Ann. What David says to his sister is evidently in reply to a prior inquiry from her. Judging by the letter's date, and the distance it had to travel, Ann would have received it just before, or possibly just after, falling into her last illness. David, as it appears, was less concerned with spelling and punctuation than with exhortation, a fairly strange custom that had grown up among the youth of the time:

To Anna Rutledge
Valued Sister. So far as I can understand Miss Graves will teach another school in the Diamond Grove I am glad to hear that you have a notion of comeing to school and I earnestly recommend to you that you would spare no time from improving your education and mind remember that "time is worth more than all gold therefore throw away none of your golden moments" I add nomore but etc.   D. H. Rutledge

To end her long morning session with Barton, Mrs. Saunders consented to have her photograph taken. Lifting her frail weight from the couch into a wheelchair, Barton "rolled her out into the sunshine and made a picture of her, the last that was taken." That same night, delighted with the outcome of his long journey, anxious to put on record what he felt was at least a minor coup in Lincoln research, Barton began writing up his story. It was promptly picked up by a wire service and routed to most large cities, many papers using it at the time or subsequently. Barton had acted none too soon. A year later, on May 1, 1922, without ever leaving Lompoc nursing home, the last of the New Salem Rutledges died.

By the mid-twenties, the three amateur historians, Beveridge, Barton, and Sandburg, had completed their Lincoln studies and were preparing to publish. But as the work of these three, in varying degrees, gained renewed attention and respect for the legend, the long-slumbering world of the professional scholar at last began to rouse itself. Rubbing the sleep from its eyes, it decided that it would take up the neglected task of testing the legend.

Beveridge, the only one of the three privileged to work with Herndon's documents, in his volume readily accepted the romance itself, wholeheartedly and uncritically, while hesitating over some aspects. Believing nearly everything said by Herndon's informants, in his well-constructed if rather too dense narrative he quoted comments from many of the supposed eyewitnesses, not so much as proof but as illustration. Between Abe and Ann he found that there had been perhaps not a formal engagement but at least a tentative agreement to marry, the wedding to take place as soon as Lincoln had gained a position in some law office. But to that conclusion he added a curious and not very clear remark that may only reflect his own subdued temperament: "Neither Ann nor Abraham it would seem displayed any precipitancy of passion." The claims relating to Lincoln's spell of insanity he passed over rather speedily, managing to create an impression that hardly more was involved than a normal and quite natural grief. Lincoln's sadness at Ann's passing, he said, was to be noted only "in his gloomy and dejected manner."

Beveridge's work gave the legend the most sustained documentary support it had received to that time. But in the view of those with a more serious concern for the truth of history he had—in his failure to provide any sort of discussion in depth or analysis of sources, and in his unsophisticated handling of the anecdotal evidence—sadly muffed his great chance. Before that chance would again arise, another twenty years were to pass.

Barton, in his volume *The Women Lincoln Loved,* also accepted the legend but with a touch of hesitation and showing signs of confusion if not actual ambivalence. After giving up on the absent McNamar, thought Barton, Ann had willingly accepted the attentions of "the awkward, raw-boned" Lincoln. But while the two had "cared for each other," there was no way to tell if they had become officially engaged. Barton wasn't even sure just how serious had been the feelings on either side, Lincoln's especially, with or without an engagement: "No one in New Salem suspected that he had loved Ann Rutledge with an incurable affection." The widespread popular notion that Abe and Ann had shared in a grand, undying union of souls amounted, he was positive, to nothing but "mushy lies." The oft-told story that the stricken Lincoln had "raved" in grief at Ann's death, had been in a despondent mood for months afterward, and had at last thought of suicide, he summarily rejected both as unproved and unlikely.

The story of Lincoln's insane spell, Barton argued, could hardly be true in any case, for another old letter had come to light that went far toward disproving it. Written by a New Salem resident, Matthew Marsh, who was a "particular friend" of Lincoln, a casual reference in it showed plainly that the sorrowing lover was back on the job, tending his regular chores at the post office, only three weeks after Ann's funeral. A chatty missive to the writer's relatives back East, dated September 17, 1835, it referred to Lincoln in his capacity as village postmaster as being "very careless about leaving his office open & unlocked during the day—half the time I go in & get my papers etc. without anyone being there as was the case yesterday.... If he is there when I carry this to the office I will get him to 'Frank' it."

Before using the Marsh letter, Barton had carefully researched the man's background, even finding that he had voted in a New Salem election just the month before. Then he promptly turned up another pertinent document, one recording the fact that, a few days after the mailing of the Marsh letter, Lincoln had done a surveying job for this same young man. As Barton insisted, the technical demands of the survey, along with Lincoln's handwriting on the plat, revealed "a clear mind" and also a "firm hand," proving that he had been in full possession of his faculties.

Interestingly, Barton's seventeen-page treatment of the legend gave to John McNamar quite as much attention as it accorded Lincoln and Ann, but in a negative way. Castigating the Scotsman as cold, selfish, and grasping, but offering no evidence, he blithely dismisses McNamar as unworthy, a man who had by remaining away so long deliberately "jilted" Ann. The reason he suggests for this also lacked support: the Scotsman had heard, somehow, that Ann's father, with the failure of the tavern, had fallen on hard times, and with that McNamar had backed out, not wanting a pauper for a wife. Sally Saunders's personal bitterness against McNamar, well founded or not, had fallen on fertile ground.

The high-water mark of the Rutledge legend's popular acceptance and development, aside from outright imaginative writing, came with Carl Sandburg's evocation of it in his vastly successful *Abraham Lincoln: The Prairie Years*. While historically correct in essentials, Sandburg's account frequently takes disconcerting liberties, crossing the line to the most blatant sort of fictional interpretation. A very human, very sensitive Lincoln, whenever he chances to gaze "into the face of the slim girl with corn-silk hair" finds himself all atremble, with "dark waves" coursing through his limbs. Talking with the girl, he cannot control the "bashful words tumbling from his tongue's end." When alone he whispers Ann's name "softly to the shadows," as he wonders if "a sucker like me can have a gal like her." The devastating depression triggered by Ann's death is described by Sandburg as a "gray mystery," a state of feeling that leads him to make frequent visits to the Concord Cemetery, "where he lay with an arm across the one grave." No doubt it is a coincidence, but it is also a fact that just a year after publication of the Sandburg excesses, with all the attention given to that work, professional historians first took up in good earnest the cry against Ann.

It was the youthful but well-qualified Paul Angle, executive secretary of the Lincoln Centennial Association, who led the scholarly counter-attack. In a sharply defined and closely reasoned article, Angle reminded his readers that the Rutledge legend was not strictly historical in character but arose entirely and unequivocally from oral tradition, and lacked even a shred of contemporary evidence. It was founded wholly on the rambling reminiscences of various unschooled persons, none collected while Lincoln lived. Without exception these late memories came either from members of the Rutledge family "or from one-time residents of New Salem interested in fastening all possible glamour on that forgotten village." The important Isaac Cogdal incident, Angle judged, was undoubtedly "spurious," Cogdal himself being no particular friend of Lincoln but "a mediocre lawyer residing twenty miles from Springfield." No one in those days ever called Lincoln "Abe," as Cogdal claimed doing, nor was it likely that a mere chance acquaintance such as Cogdal should have presumed to question the notoriously reticent Lincoln on such "intimate matters." If he had, it is certain he would have received no reply.

The Marsh letter, first used by Barton, was also taken up by Angle, who employed it with telling force to further disparage the idea of Lincoln's supposed insanity. The letter was written less than a month after Ann's death, at a time when Lincoln is supposed to have been in the depths of despair, yet it

> entertains no doubt of his ability to attend to his duties as postmaster. Moreover, when most accounts have Lincoln recuperating at the home of Bowling Green, some distance from New Salem, or at best as having just returned to New Salem from

Green's, Marsh gives no indication that he had ever been absent. True, the postmaster is somewhat careless about his office, but the correspondent very clearly implies that this carelessness is customary, and not the result of a recent emotional upheaval.

If you, in writing to your brother, were devoting an entire paragraph to "a very particular friend," would you not mention the fact that the recent death of his betrothed had plunged him into a period of near-insanity? Especially when further on in your letter you say that "there has been more sickness this summer than was ever known before"? You would—if it had.

Angle's deft thrust at the legend went home. Cogent as were his arguments, however, by themselves they might not have had so widespread and thorough an effect in alerting his colleagues to their obligation. It was another episode, wholly unlooked for, nothing less than an elaborate hoax arising at this same time and also involving Angle, that aided in fastening increasing doubts on the legend. Well known then, but now largely forgotten, the affair of the Minor forgeries was played out in full public view to its ridiculous end. By no means one of the memorable hoaxes of American history, not an integral part of the legend, its final exposure followed surely and rapidly. Yet its net effect, somewhat irrationally, was to further discredit the story of Ann and Abe.

Involving supposed letters written between the two principals, the fraud began with publication of the *Atlantic Monthly* for December 1928. Under a heading "Lincoln the Lover," the magazine excitedly announced that it had uncovered what it called a "treasure beyond price"—nothing less than a series of letters "passionate and real, which Abraham wrote to Ann, and Ann to Abraham." Brought to the magazine by a California family claiming ties to old New Salem, the letters had been, said the *Atlantic,* completely tested for authenticity before acceptance (left unstated was the relevant fact that the testing had been done largely by three earnest, and thoroughly unqualified, amateurs: Ida Tarbell, William Barton, and Carl Sandburg). Despite the fanfare, the sensation was short lived. No sooner had the letters become available in the magazine, bouyed by a good deal of convoluted explanation as to their provenance, than various professional scholars led by Paul Angle denounced them as crude forgeries. So quickly did the negative evidence pile up, particularly in the way of historical inaccuracy, that the magazine was almost immediately forced to admit its error. Angle's incisive roundup of the evidence, leaving no doubt of the forgery, was included in the *Atlantic*'s issue of April 1928, and one more Lincoln hoax came flatly to its disappointing end. Exposure of the Minor forgeries, as one leading commentator has written recently, "consigned the Ann Rutledge story to oblivion among Lincoln scholars." If it did not quite do that, it did indeed help speed the legend on its way in that direction.

                                    ᷝ

The deathblow to the fast-crumbling Rutledge legend was delivered in the year 1945, bringing a virtual end to Herndon's wildly romantic imaginings of eighty years before. So at least runs the belief current in academic circles. Fittingly enough, the damage was done by the foremost Lincoln scholar of his time, James G. Randall, who based his verdict on a most meticulous examination of the Herndon papers, which had at last been made available at the Library of Congress. Professional historians, long since fed up with the picture of an unstable, love-sick, grief-crazed Lincoln, had at last gotten what they wanted, what they had always believed to be more or less inevitable. Thereafter for nearly half a century, no respectable Lincoln scholar would permit himself to be seen in the company of the undeniably real but discredited Ann.

Considering its enormous influence, it is a curious and often overlooked fact that Randall's treatment did not provide readers with the sort of full-fledged analysis by which an independent judgment could be made. In writing up his studies he had concerned himself, as he said, only with "essential results," ignoring or brushing over most of the intermediate steps. His stated conclusion was also surprisingly circumspect. Avoiding outright condemnation, he said only that the Rutledge story must be judged "unproved," with the ultimate truth conceded to be "well nigh unrecoverable." Yet to any careful reader it was also immediately apparent that Randall, personally, would have preferred to reject the legend outright, perhaps allowing for only the most ephemeral of youthful attachments. It was that unstated background attitude, expressed in broadly roundabout terms, that stayed with his readers.

Giving the topic some twenty crowded pages in his book on Lincoln the President (but relegated to an appendix), he plainly shows his negative leanings in the opening paragraph. Where his title for the appendix declares that he will be "Sifting the Ann Rutledge Evidence"—presumably to see if it held anything that might be considered reliable—he can still frankly state that, "If one is treating only those things whose reality and significance for Lincoln are matters of solid proof, the too familiar story of Lincoln and Ann may be omitted altogether." The subject, he says, has been taken up, "not for any intrinsic importance at all, but because historical criticism finds here a challenge and a needful task. From uncertain and conflicting memories of a courtship in picturesque New Salem the story has amazingly grown until the romantic linking of Abe and Ann has become universal."

At a stroke, and before touching the evidence, Randall confesses that the old drama of Abe and Ann in his opinion has become annoyingly prevalent (the phrase "too familiar" is vague enough to mean several things, none favorable). In other words, the old story has no intrinsic value for, or place in, the Lincoln saga. It is based on fallible "memories" that, when analyzed, prove to be contradictory as well as "uncertain" (a word itself capable of notably loose meaning). The tone of the article's opening is crucial, for it quietly informs the knowledgeable reader that, whatever is said thereafter about the "evidence," the question is to be viewed from the start as settled, needing a degree of condescension even to discuss.

Combing through the testimony of some twenty of the New Salem informants, Randall is content to leave them largely unquoted and unidentified. Here and there, while the discussion proceeds in meandering fashion, he gives brief, selected phrases from their correspondence or from interviews. Only over one of the statements does he linger, that provided by Ann's brother Robert. But his purpose is still not to analyze, for almost flippantly he comments, "Here is one person reporting what another person had written him concerning what that person recollected he had inferred from something that Ann had casually said to him more than thirty-one years before!" (As will be seen further on, the word "reporting" in that passage should properly be "quoting," a significant difference, and the word "casually" does not belong there at all.)

The Isaac Cogdal incident Randall dismisses, even more curtly than did Angle, as "artificial and made to order." No real friend of Lincoln, Cogdal was only "a farmer and former brick mason who studied law late in life." Lincoln's grief at Ann's death, if true grief was felt at all, was "exaggerated by local gossip." So the catalog went, judged Randall, "some pro, some con, some inconclusive, all of it long delayed reminiscence, much of it second- or third-hand."

The conclusion of Randall's article—all the more effective since the reader has already heard the quietly assured caveats pronounced at the opening—was to dominate the question for almost the next half century:

> In its origin the Ann Rutledge story rests on wavering memories recorded many years after the event. No proved contemporary evidence is known to exist. . . . Reminiscences gathered long after the event were not all in favor of the romance; they were contradictory and vague. . . . Whatever may have been the true situation as to Lincoln and Ann, that situation seems now well nigh unrecoverable. As to a romantic attachment, it has not been *dis*proved. It is more correct to characterize it as *un*proved; as such it has been a famous subject of conjecture. It is a memory which lacks support in any statement recorded in Ann's lifetime. Since it is thus traditional and not reliably established as to its nature and significance, it does not belong in a recital of those Lincoln episodes which one presents as unquestioned reality.
>
> As a historical puzzle or an exercise in the value of reminiscence the Lincoln-Rutledge story is a choice subject; but its substance is far from clear while its fringe is to be discarded from the record of established history. By that fringe we mean the elaboration, the trimmings and embroidery, the fictional sentimentalizing, the invented poeticisms, and the amazing aura of apocryphal material that have surrounded the whole overgrown tale. . . . assuredly the effect of the episode upon Lincoln's later life has been greatly exaggerated—or rather, fabricated. Nor should one lightly overlook the shabby manner in which the image of Ann has tended to obscure the years of Lincoln's love and devotion to Mary, his wife, and to belittle her love and devotion for him.

Setting aside the merits of his argument, it is perhaps in those closing sentences about Mary Lincoln that Randall's true motivation, or a good portion of it, comes into view. Not mere scholarship alone it was that led him to brandish a spear at the legend but something far more human and admirable: a strong and active sense of chivalry. Posthumously he rushes to the defense of his hero's stricken widow, then dead some sixty years, and in that reaction even for a dedicated scholar there is nothing really strange or reprehensible. In the end it serves to highlight a fact of peculiar pertinence for the study of the Rutledge legend: James Randall, twentieth-century Lincoln student, and James Smith, nineteenth-century Lincoln pastor, are brothers.

ૐ

When the revolt against Randall finally came, it came with a bang. Within a matter of months in 1990 two professional historians published articles decrying the unearned influence of, and the damage done by, the Randall appendix. Both proceeded to proclaim, along with an effort to demonstrate, the full historical reality of the basic legend. Suddenly it was once more permissible for scholars to invoke the name of Rutledge, to wonder what might have happened if Ann had lived, to argue about the possible effects on Lincoln of his deep sorrow at her loss. The maid of old New Salem was on her way to becoming respectable again.

"Available evidence," insisted the first of the two, the experienced John Simon, "overwhelmingly indicates that Lincoln so loved Ann that her death plunged him into severe depression." Pointing to the overlooked fact that "no knowledgeable witness ever denied the affair," Simon slices away at Randall's position until, in one arrowlike sentence, he hits the target dead center. Randall, he states, impermissibly "reclassified the romance as an accusation needing proof, something of which Lincoln would be held innocent until proved guilty." Rather, it should be taken as a normal biographical incident, "about which a preponderance of reliable evidence would prevail."

The extraordinary Isaac Cogdal incident Simon neatly rescues. Stressing the friendship of the two back in their New Salem days, he shows that Lincoln even as president-elect would have been "Abe" to Cogdal, as he was and remained to all his early neighbors. Another telling fact he also ably demonstrates, that Lincoln when about to leave Springfield for the White House was definitely in the proper mood to answer Cogdal's questions: an intensely nostalgic frame of mind. Lincoln spoke openly of Ann, Simon suggests,

> because Cogdal asked, something few would have had the knowledge, opportunity, or temerity to do. Lincoln might not have

answered before his last winter in Illinois, a time when he visited his father's grave, neglected for a decade, and left Springfield saying "all the strange, chequered past seems to crowd now upon my mind." Cogdal, who may well have misrecollected Lincoln's words some half dozen years after the conversation, had no known reason to misrepresent what Lincoln said.

The second respected scholar to speak out in 1990, Douglas Wilson, also begins by refuting Randall, but he soon enters on his main theme: a poll among the old settlers who gave Herndon his information about the romance. With copies of the original documents before him, Wilson searched through letters, notes, and records of interviews to find if possible the answers given by each individual to three simple questions:

> 1. Did Lincoln love or court Ann Rutledge?
> 2. Did Lincoln grieve excessively at Ann's death?
> 3. Did they have an understanding about marriage?

Involved were twenty-four witnesses, all from in and around New Salem, all Lincoln's old friends and acquaintances. Their answers to the three questions, as gleaned from the documents, were toted up and arranged under three heads. The counts were impressive:

	Yes	No	No opinion
Question 1	22	0	2
Question 2	17	0	7
Question 3	15	2	7

Regarding the two informants who denied an actual engagement, Wilson moves quickly to point out that one of them was a child at the time. The other dissenter, an aunt of Ann who thought that her niece would have preferred McNamar to Lincoln, he does not quite succeed in explaining away. In any case, as he concludes happily, his poll has proved decisive on all three points, with the informants "overwhelmingly in agreement."

Like Simon, Wilson too provides insightful analyses of some of the individual statements, showing in particular how the Rutledge family, far from being eager for reflected glory, had "at first shied away from Herndon." Most importantly, he is able to add still further believability to the Cogdal incident. Not only had the two men been friends in their

New Salem days, points out Wilson, but they had kept in touch afterward, and it was actually Lincoln who encouraged Cogdal to take up the law. Agreeing with Simon, Wilson stresses the importance of the context of Cogdal's talk with Lincoln, and he shows how careful Cogdal was in taking advantage of it ("I then *dared* to ask him this question"). Herndon himself in speaking with Cogdal, Wilson adds, also understood how critical were the circumstances of the meeting. Pointedly he inquired of Cogdal just how, with what specific words, he had introduced the risky question into the conversation. In reply Cogdal recalled his attitude as having been quite deferential: "May I now in turn ask you a question Lincoln." Most effectively and pertinently, Wilson shows that Cogdal's memory of that day was not drawn from the dim past, for he was testifying just five or six years after the event. Further, the meeting "was not an obscure encounter with an old friend but an extremely memorable one with the President-elect of the United States."

Between them, Simon and Wilson succeeded brilliantly in reviving the Rutledge legend, making it fit once again for serious study. In their separate discussions of the claims made by a few of the individual eyewitnesses they also came near evoking some final truths in the matter. Now, in an effort to get still nearer those truths, the next logical, indeed what might be termed the ultimate, step may be taken. It is a step that might have been ventured at any point in the last fifty years (in another way this quiescent interlude should perhaps be measured at nearly three times that length). Why it was not, why the Randall view prevailed unchallenged for so long, is a curious if less urgent question that shall not be pursued here.

It is time for Lincoln's old New Salem neighbors to be recognized as the intelligent and responsible individuals they were. Having waited patiently in the wings for more than a century, they shall now be invited to take center stage. Properly introduced, they will finally be allowed the chance, one by one, to speak for themselves.

4

She Had an Angel's Heart

IN PETERSBURG in 1865 there lived a man named Hardin Bale. Then forty-nine, in his youth he had been a resident of old New Salem, where he had lived with his father, Jacob, his mother, Elizabeth, a sister, and two younger brothers. It was this man who first told Herndon about Ann Rutledge.

The Bales had come to the New Salem vicinity from Kentucky in 1830, settling first in a cabin about a mile to the northwest. A businessman more than a farmer, Jacob soon bought the faltering Rutledge gristmill on the Sangamon at the foot of the bluff, and by 1835 had installed on New Salem's main street its first carding machine. Still not content, in another year he added a loom for weaving wool. When Lincoln left New Salem for Springfield in the spring of 1837, Hardin Bale had been in charge of his father's village operations for two or three years, the same years in which the Lincoln-Rutledge story was unfolding.

In 1839 Bale married a girl from near New Salem, Esther Summers, and two years later he moved to Petersburg where he started his own mill. Whether he ever met Lincoln during the ensuing twenty years is unknown, but it is more than probable. During the forties, Lincoln was often in Petersburg on law business, some of it for the old settlers, and at least one relative of Bale, his uncle Abram, later consulted Lincoln on a law matter (he was advised to settle out of court). When Hardin and his wife left the rapidly dwindling village of New Salem in 1840 to take up residence in Petersburg, his father remained behind, among the last to leave, becoming the final owner and occupant of the Rutledge tavern. By the time Herndon spoke with the younger Bale in Petersburg, on May 29, 1865, he had become one of the town's most prosperous and respected citizens (shortly afterward, fire destroyed his mill and factory and he lost nearly everything).

Herndon, busily researching his planned biography of Lincoln, had not come to Petersburg that May expressly to interview Bale. By then the town had long served as the Menard County seat, and Herndon as usual was there to tend to several cases being tried at the spring session of the circuit court. But he had known for some time about the large Bale family and its New Salem background, was aware that Hardin and his wife would be prime sources for information on the young Lincoln. What he eventually heard from them concerning one aspect of his subject's early life must have taken him considerably by surprise.

Bale began the interview, according to Herndon's notes, and no doubt on request, by giving something of his own background. He then briefly mentioned several Lincoln items that have since become standard—his clerkship in a grocery, his service as an officer in the Black Hawk War, his great physical strength and athletic ability, his storytelling and reading habits, and his surveying. He also described Lincoln's invention of a "water-wheel," an item otherwise unknown to Lincoln lore. Then, without preparation or transition, and apparently of his own volition, Bale told the following:

> He at this time fell in love with a Miss Ann Rutledge—a pretty and much accomplished girl of Menard County, living in New Salem. It was said that after the death of Miss Rutledge & because of it, Lincoln was locked up by his friends—Samuel Hill and others, to prevent derangement or suicide—so hard did he take her death.

Herndon's notes of the interview contain no comment of his own on this unexpected news, not even recording the fact that he had himself known Ann. Having said so much, Bale went on without further comment to other, unrelated Lincoln items.

That same day (though it may have been later), Herndon talked with Mrs. Bale, uncovering still further information on Ann. As Herndon knew, Esther Bale's memories were personal, not derived from her husband, for she too had grown up near New Salem village, one of a large family, and had known Ann well. Replying to a question, she started by giving a physical description of the girl: "Miss Rutledge had auburn hair, blue eyes, fair complexion. She was pretty, slightly slender... about five feet two inches high, and weighed in the neighborhood of a hundred twenty pounds. She was beloved by all who knew her." Two additional sentences in the notes taken down from Mrs. Bale should—if Herndon was even normally inquisitive—have prompted a perfect barrage of further questioning, and yet there is no sign of it. The two sentences are simply strung together without comment or explanation: "She died as it were of grief. In speaking of her death and her grave Lincoln once said to me, 'My heart lies buried there'." That the questioner let pass in silence the provocative claim that "grief" had killed the girl, seems strange. As a lawyer, Herndon possessed years of experience at drawing people out and faithfully recording their replies. For the disturbing lacunae here, perhaps the best explanation is the obvious one, confirmed by other evidence: not all that the busy Herndon said or did, not all that he was told, found its way into his disorderly notes and files.

On his very first try, if the Bales were to be believed, Herndon had uncovered something he could hardly have anticipated, a young Lincoln so passionately in love that he had, when faced with the tragedy of loss, approached mental collapse. Except for a formal engagement, the whole basic outline of the legend was present in the less than two hundred words spoken by the Bales. How much credence Herndon may have given the story as he left the Bales' house that day cannot be known. But within hours, at the home of another old New Salem resident, he picked up his first tentative confirmation.

The only schoolmaster the little village on the bluff had known during its decade of existence was the sober-minded, aptly named Mentor Graham. Ann herself had sat in his classes, starting when she was fourteen, and his recollections of her were clear and vivid, or so he claimed. The young Lincoln, too, engaged in private study, had come to Graham for help now and then, especially when he began struggling with the mathematics of surveying. In the years since his departure from the depleted town, Graham had continued to conduct a grammar school in the Petersburg vicinity, and in 1865 when Herndon talked with him he was still going strong as a teacher in his mid-sixties—he didn't give up the classroom entirely until he was nudging eighty, nicely rounding out a career of a half century. Twice in the years after

New Salem, Graham was involved in court cases handled by Lincoln (once in a fugitive slave case where Graham was the accuser!), but there seems to have been no more personal or sustained contact between them.

Judging by the length of Herndon's notes, the Graham interview, also dated at Petersburg on May 29, lasted somewhat longer than that of the Bales. The reference to Ann, however, is much briefer and more casual, almost offhand, as if not worth lingering over. It occurred near the close of the conversation and consisted of a single veiled and fleeting phrase embedded in a short, confusing passage. Graham is talking of Lincoln's character: "He was studious—so much so that he somewhat injured his health and constitution. The continuous thought & study of the man caused—with the death of one whom he dearly and sacredly loved, a momentary—only partial and momentary derangement."

Though the notes do not reflect it, this sudden reference to an unknown sacred love was probably linked by Herndon with the Ann described earlier that day by the Bales. In addition, he could scarcely have failed to connect Graham's use of the forceful word "derangement" with Hardin Bale's downright assertion that Lincoln had been "locked up." In any case, Herndon was not yet done with Mentor Graham, who had, as it would prove, still more of consequence to say about both Abe and Ann.

ॐ

One of the first friends made by the twenty-two-year-old Lincoln on reaching New Salem in July 1831 was a young man nearly his own age, William G. Green. Though they seem never to have been actual intimates, for several years there were few men of the community who knew more about Lincoln than Billy Green. He worked as Lincoln's helper in the grocery store, marched off with him to fight Black Hawk, afterward aided his studies, and was involved with him in several small business ventures. As with Lincoln, Green too gained his education on his own, reading before the cabin fire. But he also managed to attend college and later to teach school, and then to start several businesses. By the time the inquisitive Herndon located him living in the village of Tallula, a few miles south of Petersburg, he had become the wealthy and influential head of a large family (one daughter was away at school in Germany) with interests in farming, railroading, and banking. Green was also one of only two New Salem friends of Lincoln to visit him in the White House. On that occasion Lincoln introduced Green to Secretary Seward, saying that his old friend was the man who taught him grammar. This the surprised Green promptly denied in some discomfort, saying that he had simply helped Lincoln by posing questions out of a textbook and checking the answers.

Green was also involved in one of the best-known Lincoln incidents at New Salem, the wrestling bout with Jack Armstrong of Clary's Grove. In large measure it was the youthful Green's constant boasting about his friend's prodigious strength that helped bring on the challenge, and his eyewitness description of the match remains the most reliable of the several that have come down. It was Green who remembered the essential point, that the indecisive outcome of the bout actually gained Lincoln something of far more value than the acclaim that went with victory.

As Green recalled it, after Lincoln had won the first fall—two out of three would decide—the frustrated Armstrong attempted a move that even under the rough rules of the frontier was illegal. This the angry Lincoln countered by applying a devastating choke hold of his own, also illegal, upon which Armstrong's cronies rushed in. Their intent, as Lincoln knew, was not only to rescue their man but in the process to punish his opponent. Releasing Armstrong, Lincoln backed up against a wall and growled that if they wanted a fight he was ready (by "fight" he meant not wrestling but a serious combat using fists, elbows, feet, and anything else short of actual weapons by which real damage could be inflicted). He'd take them all on, he shouted, one at a time. It was a brave performance, and it won the admiration of all present, including Armstrong. Ordering hostilities to cease, the Clary's Grove champion offered his hand to the cornered Lincoln. Shortly afterward, Lincoln's mental abilities started to become evident in the village, and it was this rare combination of physical and intellectual superiority that brought him his first recognition as thinker and leader. Lincoln himself, looking back, credited the influence of the wrestling match with opening for him the doors to political life.

Green's 1865 interview with Herndon, at Green's farm in Tallula, took place only a day after those with Bale and Graham. The notes Herndon made that day, and had Green sign, run for thirteen pages, and the section on Ann is correspondingly long, much the fullest on the topic Herndon was to obtain from a single source. Whether Green mentioned Ann on his own initiative or in reply to a direct question is not discernible. It must also be remembered that Green's words were set down by Herndon, who may have somewhat altered the shading:

> He in the years 1833 & 4 was in love with a young lady in New Salem by the name of Miss Ann Rutledge. She accepted the overtures of Lincoln and they were engaged to be married. This young lady was a woman of exquisite beauty, but her intellect was quick—sharp—deep & philosophical as well as brilliant. She had as gentle & kind a heart as an angel, full of love—kindness—sympathy. She was beloved by everybody and everybody respected and loved her—so sweet and angelic was she. Her character was more than good; it was positively noted throughout the county. She was a woman worthy of Lincoln's love and she was most worthy of his.* She was suddenly—a short time before the marriage was to be she took sick with the brain fever and died in 4 or 5 days. Lincoln went & saw her during her sickness—just before her death. Mr. Lincoln's friends after this sudden death of one whom his soul and heart dearly loved were compelled to keep watch and ward on Mr. Lincoln, he being from the shock somewhat temporarily deranged. We watched during storms—fogs—damp gloomy weather Mr. Lincoln for fear of an accident. He said "I can never be reconciled to have the snow—rains & storms to beat on her grave."

From what others reported it can be said that Ann was quite pretty, enough so to make her looks one of the things people remembered about her. Green's "exquisite beauty," however, seems an overstatement, the typical nostalgia of an old man. Still, he did know the girl, and who can be sure in such matters? Her mental abilities, too, were recalled by others as having been some way above the average. But Green was the only one who remembered her as philosophical or brilliant. What he says about her as being charmingly good-natured, "sweet and angelic," and being loved by everyone may also seem

---

*The two tautologies in this passage (the phrases beginning "beloved by everybody" and "she was a woman worthy") are obvious slips, perhaps by Green, perhaps by Herndon. Their meaning in any case is evident: Ann was a favorite of all, and she loved all in return. And Lincoln was seen as worthy of *her* love, as well as she of his.

exaggerated. But in this it can be said that Green spoke only the truth, for Ann's gentleness was repeatedly mentioned and always highly praised.

Lincoln had been dead only six weeks, and Herndon already possessed the Rutledge legend in near fullness, and on the word of four primary informants. Only lacking now was the role played by McNamar, crucial information that would take a while to surface. Meantime, still further corroboration reached Herndon, this time in the unexpected form of an old newspaper story.

Early in June 1865 a letter arrived at the Herndon home in Springfield from John Hill, editor of the *Menard Axis,* a weekly published at Petersburg. Editor Hill, as Herndon knew, was the son of Samuel Hill, then deceased, New Salem storekeeper and friend of Lincoln, the same Sam Hill mentioned by Bale the week before. John Hill, a center of information for the area, had been one of the first people contacted by Herndon, and between the two at least one letter had already passed. The present letter obviously replies to some specific questions, and it is also evident that Hill had previously told Herndon of a certain article that had been carried in the *Axis* while Lincoln was alive, just as he concluded his first year as president:

> Yours of yesterday is at hand. I will be more prompt this time. Miss Ann Rutledge died within a few days of September 1st 1835. *Certain.* Lincoln bore up under it very well until some days afterward a heavy rain fell, which unerved him and—(the balance you know).

After straying briefly into another topic, Hill then explains the background of the story in the clipping. He makes it clear that besides being the author of the piece, he also did the research for it, evidently speaking to many of the same people now being approached by Herndon:

> Enclosed I send the printed slip [clipping]. I published it in 1862. Every item in it I believe to have been true except in relation to keeping a stallion. I made good inquiry before writing & think I arrived at the truth. The order of succession may not be technically true.

The account in the clipping is headed boldly "A Romance of Reality." Some thousand words in length, it aims to tell in inspirational fashion of Lincoln's rise to the White House from poverty ("What an example of ambition for the youths of the land," etc.). Describing the hardships of Lincoln's early life (some of the information derived, it would seem, from the campaign biographies), Hill includes a rapid sketch of an ill-fated romance with an unnamed young woman:

> He now became an actor in a new scene. He chanced to meet with a lady who to him seemed lovely, angelic, and the height of perfection. Forgetful of all things else, he could think or dream of naught but her. His feelings he soon made her acquainted with, and was delighted with a reciprocation. This to him was perfect happiness, and with uneasy anxiety he awaited the arrival of the day when the twain should be one flesh. But that day was doomed never to arrive. Disease came upon this lovely beauty, and she sickened and died. The youth had wrapped his heart with hers, and this was more than he could bear. He saw her to her grave, and as the cold clods fell upon the coffin, he sincerely wished that he too had been enclosed within it. Melancholy came upon him; he was changed and sad. His friends detected strange conduct and a flighty imagination. New circumstances changed his thoughts, and at length he partially forgot that which for a time had consumed his mind.

Lincoln himself may well have seen this account, at least he may have heard of it. If so, did he perhaps link it in some way with his intimate talk with Isaac Cogdal the year before? Is it possible that the Cogdal conversation in some way gave rise to the Hill story? Legitimate questions, surely, but at the moment beyond answering.

Behind Hill's facts, as will be seen, lay not only the memories of his father and other New Salem informants but those of his mother as well. That is one of the central points in the entire Rutledge legend, for Parthena Hill had been among Ann's intimate companions, perhaps her closest.

≈

The long, shrieking call of a steamboat whistle echoed piercingly over the little village of New Salem on the afternoon of March 21, 1832, the first time the distinctive wail had sounded in the region. An undersized, low-decked vessel named *Talisman* was on its way up the Sangamon to Springfield, testing whether steamboat travel might be possible on the narrow, changeable, rather shallow waterway. If a dependable schedule could be established, then the whole region would share in the benefits of a ready access to outside markets. Involved in the daring venture was one New Salem man, James Rowan Herndon, cousin of William, and it was through Lincoln's friendship with this other Herndon that he was asked to take part in the experiment. Thirty-three years later this same Row Herndon, as he was called, would become the fifth key informant on Ann Rutledge.

Lincoln's connection with the *Talisman,* though limited, brought him again prominently before New Salemites. With Row Herndon he led the party of axe-men that preceded the slowly moving boat upriver from Beardstown on the Illinois, clearing away submerged tree trunks, rocks, overhanging branches, and other encumbrances. After four or five days, Springfield was reached, prompting great celebration, and there the boat's captain and pilot, by prior agreement, left it. For the return trip down the Sangamon to the broad Illinois, Row Herndon, an experienced riverman, became the pilot, and he chose Lincoln to assist him. The journey back was without incident, and for his work each man was paid the then large sum of forty dollars. All the sudden dreams of booming growth for the area, however, were soon to fade. While this initial experiment had been successful, a later one, defeated by the river's shifting course and uncertain levels, was a failure.

William Herndon's contact with his cousin Row in 1865 was not accomplished in person but by correspondence. It was not until Row Herndon sent a fourth letter, in fact, dated July 3, 1865, that Ann's name came up, and even then it appears only at the close of four pages. The spelling and punctuation given here follow Row Herndon's scraggly hand exactly, but these deficiencies are not to be taken as meaning a complete absence of learning, or of low intelligence. Other testimony identifies the man as thoroughly capable:

> You ask about him as regards women they all liked him and [he] like them as well. There was a Miss Rutlage I have no doubt he would have maried iff she had of lived But Deth Prevented After I left there I am told that he borded with Benett Able the farthering [*sic*] law of Nult Green I think Mrs. Able could aid you considerable she had a dauter that is thought to be Lincoln's child they favor [each other] very much. Mrs. Able is a very smart woman well educated.

That rather jolting reference to one of Elizabeth Abell's children possibly being Lincoln's is valuable in one sense, if it is worthless in another. It helps in recalling the stark reality and rawness of the frontier existence, where a sense of unusual freedom from ordinary constraints affected all sorts of people, making even speculation about the fathering of children, seriously or in jest, not uncommon. Lincoln was indeed a close friend of both Dr. and Mrs. Bennett Abell of New Salem, and he often visited them at their home just north of the village. The night Ann died, and for some days before, he was staying at their cabin, and Mrs. Abell later recalled for Herndon his strong reaction to the tragedy. But that particular bit of testimony must wait its turn.

Row Herndon was also linked, this time tragically, to another brief glimpse of Lincoln at New Salem, which also involved Ann. One of the few recollections to picture the two in company, it was preserved in the memory of Nancy Rutledge (later Mrs. Prewitt) because of a strange and fatal accident that took place in the Herndon cabin in January 1833. Many years afterward, Nancy recalled how Lincoln was at the Rutledge tavern one day, engaging in a friendly scuffle with her brother John. The horseplay was indoors and it ended with the two falling against a bed and breaking one of the cords. The apologetic Lincoln, explained Nancy, "said he must help Annie when she went to fix it next morning." As the two worked on the bed cord the following day Lincoln found that he needed a certain tool, and he sent the ten-year-old Nancy to borrow one at the nearby cabin of Row Herndon (less than two hundred feet distant from the Rutledge tavern, as the two houses are sited in present-day New Salem). What happened next must be told by Nancy:

> When I arrived there Mr. Herndon was loading his gun to go hunting, and in getting ready to go out his gun was accidentally discharged, and his wife, who was sitting near, talking to me, was shot right through the neck. I saw blood spurt out of each side of her neck, her hands flutter for a moment; then I flew out of the house and hurried home and told Annie and Mr. Lincoln what had happened. I can never forget how sad and shocked they looked, after having been so merry over their work just a moment before.

Nancy's reminiscence of the awful event was recorded in print only once, more than fifty years afterward, so it might naturally be felt that some weighty scepticism was in order. Yet here at least contemporary proof is available, and it fully supports Nancy's memory, even to the location of the fatal wound. The *Sangamon Journal,* published at Springfield, in its issue for January 25, 1833, carried the following short account:

> TERRIBLE ACCIDENT.—We learn that on Wednesday last, while Mr. R. Herndon of New Salem was preparing his rifle for a hunting excursion it went off, and the ball, striking his wife in the neck, separated one of the principal arteries, and in a few moments she was a corpse. It is hardly possible to conceive the anguish of the husband on this melancholy catastrophe. The community in which he lives deeply sympathize with him in this afflicting event.

To judge by the newspaper story, the poor woman died almost on the spot, and this fact makes peculiarly relevant and reliable Nancy's saying that she saw the wounded woman's hands "flutter for a moment." On the strength of that small detail alone it is easy to believe Nancy when she claims to have retained for half a century the linked memory of Mrs. Herndon's shocking death and her sister's merry morning with Lincoln. Another reason, perhaps, for her keeping the incident so clearly in mind, though she doesn't mention it, is the fact that the slain woman was a sister of Mentor Graham, whose daily classes Nancy was then attending.

Also to be noted in this connection is a further relevant fact. At the time of the accident, in which the evidence shows Lincoln and Ann to have been on familiar terms, John McNamar had been gone from New Salem for six months.

❧

"I saw Short, found him at Bronson's office," wrote George Miles of Petersburg to his son-in-law William Herndon. "Bronson red him your letter he took the letter home and said he would make out an answer in the course of a week." Miles's letter, dated June 28, 1865, shows that the dedicated Herndon was finally reaching toward a witness who would prove of signal importance in the Rutledge story: James Short, an old New Salemite, later of Sandridge, known to all as Uncle Jimmy. When the impoverished and struggling young Lincoln had reached what was probably the lowest point of his fortunes at New Salem and faced financial disaster, it was Uncle Jimmy who came to his rescue.

In August 1834 Lincoln won his first election, running second among thirteen candidates from Sangamon County for the Illinois legislature. Three months later, however, and before he made his political debut in the state capital at Vandalia, he suddenly and completely lost his main means of livelihood (service in the legislature barely qualified as part-time employment). Because of mounting debts left over from failed business ventures, especially the grocery store, a lawsuit had claimed all his personal possessions, which were to be disposed of at auction. Included were his riding saddle and his precious, well-nigh irreplaceable surveying instruments (his horse had already been lost for debt). The surveying business provided Lincoln with his main source of income, and without his instruments he must soon revert to the dreary life he had been trying so hard to escape, that of drifting laborer and sometime farmhand. It was at this juncture that Uncle Jimmy stepped in.

At that time, the fall of 1834, Lincoln was much in the vicinity of Short's house at Sandridge (so Short would later state). Only four years older than Lincoln, like many others at New Salem Short was greatly impressed by his friend's abilities, mental and physical ("He was the best hand at husking corn on the stalk that I ever saw"). When one day he noticed Lincoln drooping and discouraged over the loss of his instruments, and heard him saying morosely that he thought he would "let the whole thing go," meaning his budding political career, Short quietly determined to help. At the auction of Lincoln's things in November 1834—only a few days before Lincoln was to leave for Vandalia—Uncle Jimmy bid in the saddle and the surveying instruments for the sum of $120. He then presented them to the astonished Lincoln, who in his dejection had not even attended the auction.

Where the Rutledge legend is concerned, Short's residence at Sandridge is crucial. By this time, the fall of 1834, the Rutledge family, including Ann, also lived there, Mr. Rutledge having given up the tavern at New Salem in the spring of 1833. The Rutledge farmhouse, as Short explained, stood just to the south, "about a half mile from me."

Uncle Jimmy's promised written reply to Herndon in 1865 was produced right on time, for it is dated at Petersburg on July 7, some nine days after he received Herndon's inquiry through Miles. The letter consists of nine pages of reminiscences about Lincoln, including a brief reference to his salvaging of the instruments ("Mr. L. afterwards repaid

me when he had moved to Springfield"). What he has to say about
Ann Rutledge occurs halfway through the letter, and the special circumstance he describes shows that he would have had a peculiar advantage
for learning the truth—which is why his statement, confusing as it
seems, must be read with care. One date is needed in order to make
coherent the sequence of events, September 10, 1833, the day of
Short's marriage:

> Mr. L. boarded with the parents of Miss Ann Rutledge, from the
> time he went to New Salem up to 1833. In 1833 her mother
> moved to the Sandridge & kept house for me, until I got married.
> Miss R. staid at N.S. for a few months after her mother left,
> keeping house for her father and brothers, and boarding Mr. L.
> She then came over to her mother. After my marriage, the Rutledges
> lived about a half mile from me. Mr. L. came over to see me &
> them every day or two. I did not know of any engagement or
> tender passages between Mr. L. and Miss R. at the time. But after
> her death, which happened in 34 or 35, he seemed to be so
> much affected and grieved so hardly that I then supposed there
> must have been something of the kind. Miss R. was a good
> looking, smart, lovely girl, a good housekeeper, with a moderate
> education, and without any of the so called accomplishments.

The Rutledges, it is said on good evidence in addition to Short's,
gave up the tavern and moved to Sandridge about May 1833. Mrs.
Rutledge preceded the rest of the family in order to serve briefly as
Short's housekeeper (there was a blood relationship between the two,
and it may be that extra income was needed just then by the Rutledge
family). Some weeks or months later, Ann arrived. From mid-summer
1833, in other words, Ann was seldom seen at New Salem, a fact that
links itself to another passing remark in the Short letter. After he had settled in at Sandridge, says Short, "Mr. L. was at my house very much—
half the time." The territory assigned Lincoln by the county surveyor lay
to the north of New Salem and included Sandridge, so no doubt his presence at Short's place was often only for the convenience of an overnight stay while working in the vicinity. But Short implies that Lincoln's
visits were more frequent than that, so it is well to recall that Ann lived
only a leisurely ten-minute walk, a half mile, from the Short home.
    There is one puzzle in the Short statement, his saying he was
unaware of an engagement or even "tender passages" between his

friend and his close neighbor. If other people, apparently with less opportunity, knew of an engagement, how is it that the well-placed Short could have remained in ignorance of it? A question of equal force is this: Why was Short, once he saw Lincoln's great grief, so ready to believe that there *had* been an engagement, or "something of the kind"? In their proper place below, answers to both questions are attempted. Here it may be suggested that what Short really meant was this: while Ann lived, he was not *told* of any formal engagement by either of the two principals, both his close friends.

୫

Herndon's opening burst of research on Ann Rutledge, lasting some five weeks, was now done. During the second half of 1865 he set her aside while he pursued other aspects of Lincoln's early life, at one point making an extended journey to sites in Indiana and Illinois where he talked with, among others, Lincoln's stepmother. That same November he prepared and delivered at Springfield three lengthy and well-received lectures on Lincoln, principally an attempt to unfold his complex character. Only at the start of 1866 did he come back to the Rutledge romance—while still tracing a variety of other Lincoln threads—and he soon found himself uncovering still further pertinent information.

One of Lincoln's oldest New Salem friends was Henry McHenry, of Clary's Grove, who had married the sister of wrestling champion Jack Armstrong. Almost certainly McHenry was among the part of the Armstrong gang that had angrily closed in on Lincoln at the end of the famous bout, and the subsequent friendship between the two seems to have been fairly close. McHenry's daughter, Parthena Jane, later asserted that she had been named by Lincoln himself at the invitation of her parents, which could easily be true. More relevant is the McHenrys' leaving Clary's Grove and moving to a farm at Sandridge where they became neighbors of the Rutledges, and where they were living when Ann died. This proximity makes the letter McHenry wrote Herndon on January 8, 1866—replying to a note from Herndon of the month before—of particular value. One passage in it is obviously the prime source for Herndon's portrait of the abstracted Lincoln soliloquizing his way through the woods:

As to the condition of Lincoln's mind after the death of Miss R. After that event he seemed quite *changed,* he seemed Retired, &

loved solitude, he seemed wraped in *profound thought,* indifferent to transpiring events, had but little to say, but would take his gun and wander off in the woods by himself, away from the association of even those most esteemed.[*] This gloom seemed to deepen for some time, so as to give anxiety to his friends in regard to his mind. But various opinions obtained as to the cause of his change. Some thought it was an increased application to his law studies. Others that it was deep anquish of Soul (as he was all soul) over the loss of Miss R. My opinion is, & was, that it was from the latter cause.

The McHenry letter was followed by an unexpected communication from Herndon's Petersburg assistant, his father-in-law, George Miles. Taking it on himself to visit three elderly ladies then residing in Petersburg, all former residents of New Salem, he had plied them with questions and now had some interesting, if disappointingly brief, results to report. Nancy Green, wife of the deceased Bowling Green, had told him that "Mr. Lincoln was a regular suiter of Miss Ann Rutledge for between two & 3 years." She also recalled Lincoln's grief at Ann's death as being so marked that some of the villagers "thought his mind would become impaired." When her husband brought Lincoln home to rest, the Greens "kept him a week or two and succeeded in cheering him up though he was quite melancholy for months."

It was in Miles's further report of what Nancy Green had to say that the final necessary bit of evidence—the name of Ann's first lover—fell into place. Mrs. Green was of the opinion, wrote Miles, that Lincoln and Ann would have married well before her death "had it not been that she had another Beau by the name of John McNamar who she thought as much of as she did of Lincoln to appearance." Herndon may have encountered the name of McNamar before this, perhaps only in conversation, but in any case it was now safely written into the record. Soon he found that the man was not only still alive but was still cultivating the Sandridge farm where Ann had died. There on his farm McNamar had lived for thirty years after his return from New York, while marrying twice (his first wife died) and raising a large family.

---

[*]McHenry was probably wrong about Lincoln having a gun on these excursions, unless for protection. By his own word, Lincoln did no hunting after late boyhood.

The second and third of the three ladies who talked with Miles (separately, it is assumed) managed to contradict each other. Ann's aunt Elizabeth, the wife of her father's brother William, admitted to being well acquainted with the circumstances of her niece's romance, and with one exception she supported all that Nancy Green had said. The exception, building on the hint dropped by Mrs. Green, managed to impose on the story an unexpected twist: if Ann had lived, "she would have married McNamar, or rather she thinks that Ann liked him a little the best, though McNamar had been absent in Ohio for near two years."* It is a provocative statement, though how it fits into the picture of Ann's dual engagement is less clear—the pity is that the woman was never questioned further. The two years she specifies may be the crux. During the first year of McNamar's absence, Ann probably held her affection for him unchanged, at least felt herself bound by her promise. When that absence reached as it did toward two years, and Lincoln pressed his suit, no doubt there came the change of heart.

The last of the three ladies was Parthena Hill, Sam's wife and John's mother, who apparently chose to say little at this time. In general she agreed with the other two women but demurred on the matter of Ann's preference. "Lincoln would have got her," she told Miles, "& it was so generally believed." Somewhat later she would have considerably more to say.

---

*Confusing references to Ohio, rather than New York State, as the place of McNamar's long sojourn away from New Salem, fueled by this as well as other mentions, have cropped up in treatments of the story from the start. Some writers solve the problem by having McNamar lying ill of fever for months in Ohio before going on to New York. The fact is that McNamar's home in New York State lay in a section of Broome County then known as New Ohio. It was located some dozen miles northeast of Binghamton, nearly at the present North Colesville. Obviously, McNamar told as much to his friends at New Salem, who remembered it wrongly.

5

Lincoln Told Me So

AT FIRST, John McNamar proved a disappointment. Asked point-blank about the Lincoln-Rutledge story, he denied knowing anything, refusing even to answer questions on his long-ago acquaintance with Lincoln. The refusal, which took by surprise Herndon's emissary George Miles, occurred at the McNamar farm in Sandridge late in April 1866. Initially, McNamar had declined even to read Herndon's letter of inquiry, handed him by Miles, declaring that he "knew nothing of the matters you wish to know." Persisting, Miles at last persuaded him to read the letter. Then, upon further urging, McNamar agreed to think about writing an answer, and two weeks later it arrived at Miles's home. It was a single sheet written on both sides, in effect repeating the claim of ignorance and saying little else.

Addressed to Miles in Petersburg, the letter was dated May 5, 1866. That same day Miles sent it, with a note recording McNamar's hesitancy, to Herndon in Springfield. Declaring that he can be of little help since he was absent from New Salem during the period in question, only now and then thinking to employ a period or comma, in quite leisurely style McNamar goes on:

I left here in 32 and went to the State of New York for the purpose of assisting my Father's family my coming west being principally to obtain the means I did not go by steamboat or stage if that has anything to do with the matter but rode Old Charley a hero of the Black Hawk War who had one grievous fault—he would go to sleep occasionally fall on his nose and pitch me over his head which occasioned some profanity no doubt about it. Circumstances beyond my control detained me much longer away than I intended.

Mr Lincoln was not to my knowledge paying any particular attention to any of the young ladies of my acquaintance when I left. There was no rivalry between him and myself on that score on the contrary I had every reason to consider him my personal friend until like Andy Johnson's Tailor Partner in Tennessee, I was left so far behind in his rapid and upward strides to that imperishable fame which justly fills a world that I did not deem myself entitled to further notice.

I corrected at his request some of the Grammatical errors in his first address to the voters of Sangamon Co. his principal hoby being the navigation of the Sangamon River, the first time he presented himself as a candidate for the legislature. This production is no doubt to be found in some of the old files of the Journal.

I never heard any person say that Mr Lincoln addressed Miss Ann Rutledge in terms of courtship neither her own family nor my acquaintances otherwise. I heard simply this expression from two prominent gentlemen of my acquaintance and personal friends that Lincoln was grieved very much at her death. I arrived here only a few weeks after her death I saw and conversed with Mr Lincoln I thought he had lost some of his former vivacity he was at the post office and probably postmaster he wrote a deed for me which I still hold and prize not only for the land it conveys but as a valued memento.

Miss Ann was a gentle Amiable Maiden without any of the airs of your City Belles but winsome and comely withal a blond in complexion with golden hair, "cherry red Lips and a bonny Blue Eye."

Plainly, the Scotsman was no unlettered farmer. Just as plainly, and for whatever reason, he did not intend to give out any information beyond what seemed necessary or unavoidable. The "circumstances," for instance, that had kept him away from New Salem "much longer" than planned are quickly passed over, yet they refer to quite a lengthy period. Most surprising was his assertion that on his return to New

Salem after Ann's death no one in the village bothered to mention
what had happened during his absence between his friend and his
fiancée (implied in McNamar's statement, of course is Ann's own failure
to write him about her altered feelings).

Worthy of special note is McNamar's saying that he helped Lincoln
with his "first address to the voters." That now famous document, of
fair length at fifteen hundred words, was published in the *Sangamon
Journal* for March 9, 1832. Since it must have been in preparation for
some weeks, its start is put in early February, or more likely January or
even December, which attests a very early beginning for the friendship.
If Lincoln indeed invited McNamar's editorial assistance—it would be a
strange claim to make were it not true to some extent—he must have
had considerable respect for the Scotsman's talent and good sense.
McNamar's owning a volume of Shakespeare would have been enough
in itself to impress Lincoln, then himself eagerly reading the plays
wherever he could find a set.

A good guess as to the identity of McNamar's "two prominent
gentlemen" who described Lincoln's grief would be Samuel Hill and
Dr. John Allen, both of them friends and business partners of McNamar.
Apparently McNamar felt no concern or curiosity at the time or later
over just why Lincoln should have grieved so deeply at Ann's death,
why he became so markedly subdued.

Herndon, anxious to take advantage of what seemed a rare opening,
on receiving McNamar's letter immediately wrote again. Several more
weeks passed in silence, and then early in June there came a second
letter from the Scotsman. This time there were two sheets, written on
both sides, but containing even less about Lincoln and Ann than
before. Further, McNamar now appeared to deny his own engagement
to Ann:

> I received your very flattering letter some time since. You entirely
> overrate my ability to give you any further information concern-
> ing Mr. Lincoln's intercourse with the young ladies. I was absent
> from 32 to 35, during which time the sayings or doings of Mr.
> Lincoln have not been reported to me further than I have already
> informed you. I would remark that at that time I think neither
> Mr. Lincoln nor myself were in a situation to enter into what Mr.
> Seward would call "entangling alliances."
>
> My acquaintance with Mr. Lincoln commenced at old or as it
> was fancifully called New Salem. Whether those who named it

had had any reference to the place where the Priesthood forever after the order of Melchisedeck was declared, I am not prepared to say. The founders and builders of the old mill there were John M Cameron, who was a preacher and Mr. James Rutledge both belonging to the Cumberland Presbyterian persuasion. Mr. Cameron is or was early this spring alive he lives in California and came from Georgia. I have forgotten what state the Rutledges came from I believe he claimed some connection with the Rutledges of the Carolinas.

Miss Ann Rutledge and her father both died on the farm where I now reside and then owned. It formerly belonged to Mr. Cameron, the Rutledge farm joining it on the south. Some of Mr. Lincolns corners as Surveyor are still visible on lines traced by him on both farms. The deaths of both Mr. Rutledge and Ann occurred in 35....

Lincoln I think had not returned from the Black Hawk War when I left I cant recall seeing him for some considerable time previous more over I recollect meeting several Cadets at Columbus O. on their way to the scene of that remarkable campaign.

The last time I ever saw Mr. Lincoln was at Petersburg at the time of the Great Senatorial campaign between him and Mr. Douglas after he was done speaking he passed among his old acquaintants and gave each a cordial shake of the hand me among the rest calling me by name. I fear this will not be very satisfactory. The rise and fall of old Salem cannot interest you much.

If McNamar's memory served him well, then the date of his departure from New Salem for his trip home to New York may be pretty certainly stated. Lincoln, as is known, returned from his three-months' service against Black Hawk in mid-July 1832, probably by the 18th, definitely by the 24th. On the 26th McNamar, as is shown by a deed executed on that date, was still in town but of course was busy preparing for his departure. Since he did not see Lincoln before he left for New York—on this he is definite—it appears that he must have gone from New Salem within a very few days, say by early August. Since he also claims to have reached New Salem on his return "a few weeks" after Ann's death, the true length of his absence may be definitely stated as three full years, plus several weeks. Depending on the duration of Ann's illness—it could have been as much as a month—he was probably already on his return road when she fell sick.

Herndon, perhaps admitting to himself that he was unlikely to get from McNamar anything further on Ann by mail, now decided to test his correspondent's memory face to face. After the fall session of the circuit court in Petersburg, he would pay a personal visit to the secluded Sandridge farm.

ᘌ

When Ann died at the age of twenty-two she was, according to her teacher Mentor Graham, again attending school and was a "tolerably good schollar in all the common branches including grammar." Those words were taken down by William Herndon at another interview with the schoolmaster, held in Petersburg in the spring of 1866. Valuable as the information is (was Ann being tutored for entrance to the college at Jacksonville, in line with what her brother had written in that postscript?), it was not the most significant result of this second talk between the two. That distinction belongs to another phrase Herndon set down further along in his notes, and which makes Graham's role particularly vital: he may have been the only New Salemite to have had intimate knowledge about the love affair and the engagement that was gained directly from both principals.

Herndon's loose jottings of what was said by Graham more than hint that the teacher's statements were actually made, not in the running, slap-dash manner to be seen in the notes, but as separate replies to specific questions carefully framed by the experienced lawyer. If so, then the actual, unrecorded questions that elicited such an intermittent string of answers as the following are not hard to imagine: "Lincoln and she were engaged—Lincoln told me so—She intimated to me the same." That particular interchange may perhaps be reconstructed as:

Q. What was the nature of the friendship between Abe and Ann?
A. "Lincoln and she were engaged."
Q. How do you know that?
A. "Lincoln told me so."
Q. Did Ann say anything about the engagement?
A. "She intimated to me the same."

All of Herndon's interviews were recorded in the same hurried and staccato, even jumbled style, the inevitable result of running together only the replies. It is only by thinking back through these interviews, picturing them in progress as being conducted in a controlled and objective manner, that their true worth and weight may be gauged. That suggestion is pointedly made at this juncture because it will have clear application to what follows, an extended look at the troublesome Isaac Cogdal interview of 1866.

The second Graham interview was also worthwhile for the details it added to the growing portrait of Ann personally. Asked to describe her, he responded that she was of a fair complexion with "sandy" hair but "not flaxen," a mouth that was "well-made, beautiful," with good teeth, and eyes that were "blue large & expressive." She stood about five feet four, Graham said, weighed about 125 pounds, and was a neat if plain dresser. Until her final sickness she enjoyed good health generally: "vigorous" was how he put it.

ₐₐ

When he was twenty-two, Isaac Cogdal, called Ike by his New Salem neighbors, bought his first piece of farmland, a few acres of prairie in Rock Creek Precinct just to the north. Survey of the purchase, as the records show, was made by his friend of three years' standing, Abe Lincoln. That was in 1834, and Cogdal was to recall that even earlier, in July 1831, he had been among the first to welcome the young Lincoln to the area, actually during "the first week he came to town."

Described as "a tall, good-looking man ... an all-around man," Cogdal worked for years as a stone and brick mason, until an accident in a quarry, apparently a premature blast, deprived him of his left arm. It may have been this misfortune that led him, about the mid-1850s, to follow Lincoln's advice and study for the law—and it seems certain from the evidence that at least part of his studies were done in Lincoln's own office. Admitted to practice in Illinois in 1860, he rapidly made a mark as an attorney "of ability and high standing." He had married young, but his wife died within a decade, and by the time Herndon spoke with him in 1866 he had been married to his second wife for many years. Of the five children born to his first marriage, three had survived, and his second wife gave birth to another.

Herndon, as is known, was acquainted with Cogdal before the

interview. But his first hint that Cogdal might be the possessor of privileged information on the Rutledge story came to him in a letter of August 1866 from another friend, B. F. Irwin of Pleasant Plains. Confirming the love story of Lincoln and Ann, Irwin adds casually: "Lincoln told Isaac Cogdal all about this in the secretary's office in 1860." A second letter from Irwin a month later repeats—rather insistently, as if Herndon had raised some question—that Lincoln did in fact say to Cogdal "that he really did love the woman in 1834 and loved her still in 1860 and could not help it." Urged on by this downright claim, Herndon made sure of seeing Cogdal at his first opportunity, which came at the close of the Menard County Circuit Court's fall 1866 hearing. Cogdal's home in Rock Creek was some miles south of Petersburg, where the court sat.

When recounted in the bare, flat style of Herndon's choppy notes, the Cogdal episode has usually, and in a way understandably, prompted suspicion. To many readers Cogdal seems to be "remembering" a good deal more in this unadorned telling than was actually said at his meeting with the president-elect (granting that such a meeting occurred). In Herndon's own biography of Lincoln the air of reality is slightly improved by his setting the story in the context of several other sentimental farewell visits to Lincoln by old friends. But no biographer since Herndon has cared to give the episode extended notice, and as a consequence none has handled it well. Only in the recent articles by John Simon and Douglas Wilson is Cogdal's account accepted implicitly, the conversation between the two men viewed as natural. Since on its face the Cogdal anecdote is potentially the most consequential of all those with links to the Rutledge legend, it deserves what it has never yet received, the fullest possible analysis line by line, even word by word. The starting point must be an effort to fix more precisely just when the meeting took place.

The election of 1860 was held on November 6, and Lincoln left Springfield for Washington on the following February 11. Between these two dates he occupied various temporary offices in Springfield where he conducted business and welcomed a stream of politicians, office-seekers, and well-wishers. It was toward the close of this extended waiting period that his personal friends came to say good-bye and to wish him godspeed in the daunting task that lay ahead. No complete list was kept of these unofficial visitors, but the name of at least one other besides Cogdal can be given, a man in fact with a relation to

Lincoln very much like that of Cogdal. Erastus Wright of Springfield had also known Lincoln in New Salem days, and in his diary he records his own meeting with the president-elect.

According to Wright's diary, Lincoln opened the conversation that day by promptly bringing up associations long past: "The first time I saw you," said Lincoln to Wright, "was at the Sangamon River where I was at work on a flatboat, and you came along assessing the county." Wright responded that he remembered the incident well, and in his diary he described the young Lincoln at work with "boots off, hat, coat and vest off. Pants rolled up to his knees and shirt wet with sweat and combing his fuzzy hair with his fingers as he pounded away on the boat." The memories of both men on that occasion proved accurate, for the scene they recalled is the now familiar one of Lincoln, with his stepbrother and John Hanks, building a flatboat at Sangamo Town more than thirty-five years before.

The memories prompted by Wright, of course, are not the same sort of very personal and intimate recollections claimed by Cogdal. Yet they are of a similar nostalgic cast, reinforcing the assertion that in these final days of his Springfield life Lincoln fell into a deeply sentimental and retrospective mood. The few affecting words he spoke to the crowd from the rear of the train on the day of his departure well exemplify that mood, especially his emotional confession of "the oppressive sadness I feel at this parting" and his admission that his mind was crowded by the "strange, chequered past." There was also his heartfelt mention to the crowd at the station of the quarter century "I have lived among you . . . from my youth until now I am an old man." Calling himself old at age fifty-one is perhaps still another sign of his feelings at the time.

Even in the ordinary course, it seems, Isaac Cogdal felt himself close enough to Lincoln—in some sense his mentor in the law—so that he hardly ever hesitated in posing personal questions. A year before the presidential election, Cogdal was visiting in Lincoln's law office, with Herndon himself present, when the talk got around to matters of religion. Cogdal's own account of this earlier conversation was set down in a lengthy letter of 1874. It shows how differently his talk with Lincoln about Ann might have sounded if recorded by himself, rather than being preserved only in Herndon's galloping style:

I think it was in 1859 that I was in Lincoln's office in Springfield, and I had a curiosity to know his opinions or belief religiously;

and I called on him for his faith in the presence of W. H. Herndon. At least Herndon was in the office at the time. Lincoln expressed himself in about these words: He did not nor could not believe in the endless punishment of any one of the human race. He understood punishment for sin to be a Bible doctrine; but that the punishment was parental in its object, aim, and design and intended for the good of the offender; hence it must cease when justice is satisfied. He added all that was lost by the transgression of Adam was made good by the atonement, all that was lost by the fall was made good by the sacrifice. And he added this remark, that punishment being a provision of the gospel system, he was not sure but the world would be better off if a little more punishment was preached by our ministers, and not so much pardon for sin. I then in reply told Mr. Lincoln he was a sound Universalist and would advise him to say little about his belief, as it was an unpopular doctrine, though I fully agreed with him in sentiment. Lincoln replied that he never took any part in the argument or discussion of theological questions. Much more was said, but the above are the ideas as advanced by Lincoln there.

It may not be precisely so, but this letter seems to confirm another impression, that Lincoln simply *liked* Cogdal, liked him as someone to talk with, liked exchanging ideas with him. Where Lincoln is quoted, correctly, as saying he always avoided religious argument, in this instance he seems to have deliberately put aside his wariness of it in order to accommodate his friend.

Too often overlooked in regard to Cogdal's 1860 visit with President-elect Lincoln is the fact that it was Lincoln who invited his friend to call, not Cogdal who presumed to call. Further, judging by Lincoln's desire to review "old times and old acquaintances," it was Lincoln's purpose from the start to explore the past with his visitor. The conversation in any case, according to the notes, opened with Lincoln's asking as to the whereabouts of some well-remembered New Salem families. For a coherent view of what happened next, Herndon's quick notes must be taken piecemeal:

After we had spoken over old times—persons—circumstances—in which he showed a wonderful memory, I then dared to ask him this question. . . .

Two things in that short but thought-packed phrase stand out as of signal interest. First, Lincoln revealed a marked ability to recall in detail both the individuals and the events of thirty years before, so much so that Cogdal was surprised and impressed by it. This in turn suggests that Lincoln even before the meeting had begun calling back to memory the details of his New Salem life, privately or in talks with others such as Erastus Wright. Second, the words "dared to ask" show how keenly aware was Cogdal of the risk he incurred by bringing up the old love affair. He knew very well that he might be pushing matters too far with the normally reticent Lincoln, and yet he decided to take the chance. Support for this view of Cogdal's awareness—and sensitivity—is available in some added words that Herndon penciled along the left-hand margin of his notepaper. They show that Herndon himself had in mind the very doubts later expressed by scholars, and that he took time to press Cogdal, asking to hear just *how*, in what precise terms, the ticklish subject of Ann Rutledge was raised. Cogdal recalled his own question to Lincoln as, "May I now in turn ask you one question Lincoln." Herndon then requested the exact words of Lincoln's response. As written in the margin, Cogdal recalled them as, "Most assuredly. I will answer your question if a fair one with all my heart."

To appreciate what Lincoln meant by a "fair" question, it must be understood that as president-elect he had a duty to be circumspect. Daily he was being bombarded, by anxious visitors and by the press, with all sorts of leading inquiries about his view of governmental concerns, especially the looming rebellion. Here, he gently warns Cogdal that he must not presume on this wider arena, but that he is eager to talk—"with all my heart"—about old friends and old times.

To this point in their talk it appears that Lincoln led the conversation, which was to be expected. Now Cogdal, diffidently, almost apologetically, asks permission to bring up a subject on his own, and the real interest of the situation at this juncture lies in another urgent question, one never yet posed: *why* did Cogdal at this meeting feel impelled to ask about Lincoln's old romance? What was it that brought the memory of Ann, then dead twenty-five years, suddenly to the surface? In the absence of any clear indication, probability may be invoked, and here speculation quickly suggests an obvious answer: Cogdal's concern with Ann's tragic story was not his alone. Curiosity on the topic, prompted by Lincoln's now exalted position, may have been strongly revived among his old associates in the neighborhood. The reason for the revival is also apparent. It was not so much Ann herself who held the center of attention for these people, not just sentimental gossip about a president's old love. Much more likely, it was the recurring rumor about the young Lincoln's supposed "crazy spell," set off by the girl's death, that now gripped people's attention. What American citizen of 1860—while the very existence of the Union trembled in the balance—could be quite comfortable with the idea that the man who was to take the helm of the troubled nation had in his youth suffered a severe mental breakdown, the cause of which still burdened his restless spirit? All knew that the myriad cares and corrosive tensions awaiting the new president promised to sit more terribly on him than had even the personal tragedy of one young woman's premature death.

That by 1860, and perhaps much earlier, there was talk freely circulating about Abe and Ann in the Springfield-Petersburg area, with emphasis on Lincoln's radically unstable behavior at her death, would not be surprising. Nor in that case need it be judged out of the ordinary that Cogdal seized his chance to come away from their meeting with something definite on the question. Yet as one of the area's leading lawyers, he knew better than to probe too directly, too abruptly. Instead, he began by testing Lincoln's mood, his willingness to advert at all to the topic: "Abe is it true that you fell in love with and courted Ann Rutledge"? Even this seems too suddenly intrusive, and Herndon may have ineptly telescoped a subtler query. But what matters is Lincoln's reply to the question, which Cogdal portrays as entirely unreluctant:

> It is true—indeed. I did. I have loved the name of Rutledge to this day. I have kept my mind on their movements ever since, & love them dearly.

This candid reply would have signaled Cogdal that Lincoln was in a susceptible frame of mind, and he now ventured to pose the crucial question. But he did so rather cleverly, in a softer, more oblique way and employing the most disarming of words: "Abe—is it true that you ran a little wild about the matter?" In that delicate situation, for that sole purpose, the blithe words "ran a little wild" could hardly be improved. Responding to them, Lincoln was free to choose any tack he wished, from the briefly wistful to the heavily somber. He settled, it appears, on something in between:

I did really—I ran off the track: it was my first. I loved the
woman dearly and sacredly. She was a handsome girl—would
have made a good loving wife—was natural and quite intellectual,
though not highly educated—I did honestly and truly love the
girl and think often—often of her now.

Here indeed was "extraordinary candor," as one commentator styled
Lincoln's reply, all the more so when coming from a man at that
moment in Lincoln's position. As he is about to take office, the
president-elect confesses that he not only "ran off the track" at the
death of an old love but avers that he still thinks of the dead girl
"often—often." To grasp the true gravity of that straightforward reply it
need only be imagined as happening at the present day and somehow
reaching press and public. What heated arguments, what an uproar
would follow! What loud demands there would be to know just what
was meant by "ran off the track"!

For whatever reason, Cogdal himself took a less alarming view of
what Lincoln may have intended by that phrase. In a short notation on
a separate sheet of notepaper (made by Herndon at this first interview
or a later one, and seldom quoted), Cogdal gives his own conclusion
that "if Mr. Lincoln was crazy it [was] only technically so—and not
radically and substantially so." Rather than being insane, truly unbalanced,
thought Cogdal, Lincoln for a time after Ann's death was "terribly
melancholy—moody." Presumably, when he returned from his talk
with Lincoln he spread that same opinion among his concerned friends
in Petersburg.

One of those friends was John Hill, editor of the *Menard Axis*. Just
a year later in the *Axis* appeared Hill's inspirational article on young
Lincoln, "A Romance of Reality," with its veiled reference to Ann. In
talking of Lincoln's grief at the girl's death, Hill does not use the words
"crazy" or "insane" or any equivalent of them, nor does he so much as
hint at suicide. He says only that Lincoln was saddened and changed
and for a while acted strangely. This altered behavior Hill wraps up in a
single word: Cogdal's "melancholy."

※

With notebook in hand, as he wrote later, Herndon in October
1866 at the close of the fall session of the circuit court, went

determinedly "in search of facts" to the farm of John McNamar in Sandridge. The day of the visit was Sunday, October 14, the time ten o'clock in the morning. Arriving there, Herndon was pleased to find the farm—the same one on which Ann had died—to be quite prosperous, "well cultivated and well stocked." Cordially received, he did not forget that his purpose in going to the farm was, as he said, a "truly delicate one." Though he knew McNamar, possibly from as far back as New Salem days, the two were no more than chance acquaintances.

In person McNamar proved to be much more amenable than he had been by mail, a change perhaps brought on by talk of the many mutual friends the two found they shared in and around Petersburg (McNamar would have had distinct memories of Herndon's New Salem cousins). The visit was opened by Herndon asking about Ann's death, whether her sad end had indeed come in the house in which they were sitting. This brought from McNamar, then nearing his sixtieth birthday, an unexpectedly tender reaction as he explained that the old house where Ann had died was no longer standing:

> He sat by the open window, looking westerly, and pulling me closer to himself, looked through the window and said: "There by that"—choking up with emotion, pointing his long forefinger, nervous and trembling, toward the spot—"there, by *that* currant bush, she died. The old house in which she and her father died is gone."

Asked the date of the girl's death, McNamar readily replied August 1835 but did not name the day. There ensued some further conversation, left annoyingly unrecorded, but which no doubt largely concerned Ann and which deepened the older man's mood of "sadness." Probably something of the engagement itself was talked about—there is some evidence that McNamar, no doubt to spare the feelings of his own wife and children, imposed on his questioner a pledge of silence regarding this aspect of the story. Covered only in passing was the reason of McNamar's remaining away so long from his patient fiancée, something he was never to explain adequately.

"I left behind me in New York," he told his guest, slightly expanding on what he had written in his letters, "my parents and brothers and sisters. They [were] poor and were in more or less need when I left them in 1829. I vowed that I would come west, make a fortune, and go back to help them." He changed his name because he feared that if his family had known where he was "they would have settled down on him, and before he could have accumulated any property would have sunk him beyond recovery." What delayed his return to New Salem was the illness and death of his father, followed by the demands of his duty to help care for the remaining family. There is no sign that Herndon found the excuse for the name change to be what it was, decidedly lame (worry over the disappearance of a son on the frontier could hardly have made life easier for the struggling parents), or that he bothered to probe further into the true reasons for the three-year absence.

"Where was Ann buried?" Herndon next inquired.

"In Concord burying ground," McNamar replied, "one mile southeast of this place." But he was not precisely sure, he admitted, just where in the cemetery Ann's grave could be found, indicating perhaps that it was unmarked. By way of explaining his failure, he volunteered the information that his mother was also buried in the Concord ground (she had come back with him from New York and had died in 1845) and that the site of her grave too had been lost. The cause, in addition to his own admitted neglect, as he expressed it, was the "rapid filling up of the graveyard and the rank growth of vegetation."

It was just after eleven A.M. when Herndon left the McNamar house to drive his buggy the short distance to the Concord cemetery. Arriving there he saw on the brow of a low hill the "little white meeting house" described by McNamar, where services were just concluding. Soon he had located Samuel Berry, brother-in-law of Ann's elder sister, Jean (who had herself died only two months before). Ann's grave, Berry told him, lay next to that of her brother David, which could be identified by its headstone: "I went from the neat little church to the Concord burial ground, and soon found the grave of Miss Rutledge." Standing beside the grave, Herndon gazed a while at his surroundings. Then he found a blank page in his notebook and wrote:

The cemetery contains about one acre of ground, and is laid out in a square. The dead lie in rows, not in squares as is usual.... An extensive prairie lies west, the forest north, a field on the east, and timber and prairie lie on the south. In this lovely ground lie the Berrys, the Rutledges, the Clarys, the Armstrongs, the Jones's, old and respected citizens, pioneers of an early day.... Ann Rutledge lies buried north of her brother, and rests sweetly on his left arm, angels to guard her.

6

The Rutledges Speak

MARY RUTLEDGE, mother of Ann, in twenty-one years gave birth to ten children, of whom Ann was the third. When Abraham Lincoln died in April 1865, six of the ten were still living, three girls and three boys. Also on hand was Mary Rutledge herself, aged seventy-eight and in good health but starting to have trouble with her eyes (she would survive to ninety-one and would be blind for her final decade).

Following the death of her husband James, only three months after the loss of Ann, life grew very hard for Mary Rutledge, especially on the death in 1842 of another son, David. But while having to make several moves with her large family, always further west, she strove to keep her sons and daughters together as they grew and to allow them some chance to prosper. How well she succeeded may be read on the tall granite monument raised to her memory by her grateful children. "Oh Mother dear, a short farewell," reads the inscription, "that we may meet again above, and roam where angels love to dwell."

Of the six Rutledge children alive in 1865, three of them—John, Nancy, and Robert, all married and raising families—resided along with their mother some 150 miles to the west of Springfield in two small Iowa towns, Burlington and Birmingham. Two others had remained in or returned to Petersburg and its vicinity: the eldest, a girl named Jean, then married to James Berry, and William, married and the father of four. The sixth, Sarah (or Sally), by then had gone to California with her own growing family. Also in Petersburg, a long-time resident, was James McGrady Rutledge, the man who had been Ann's favorite cousin.

All these Rutledges, near and far, were to be pursued by the relentless Herndon, though not so promptly as might have been expected.

For some reason, it was not until the late summer of 1866, more than a year after he had first uncovered Ann's name, that Herndon made any attempt to contact the Rutledge family. Having known them at New Salem, it can hardly be said that he was unaware of the existence, if not the whereabouts, of at least some of Ann's brothers and sisters, and even brief inquiry must have turned up some addresses or other leads. Of course, there was the six-month interruption to Herndon's local research in the latter part of 1865, after which he was for a while busily engaged in catching up with his neglected professional duties. It is too easy in trailing after Herndon on his Rutledge quest to overlook how much else was on his mind through it all, including business and family cares. No doubt he also now and then just ran out of energy, his natural enthusiasm flagging. As matters developed, when he did at last reach the Rutledges, they proved to be helpful and welcoming. They also showed themselves quite level-headed, by no means eager for what promised to be reflected glory (indeed, McGrady Rutledge at first quietly repulsed Herndon's overtures).

Spokesman for the family was Robert, a brother five years younger than Ann. Aged forty-six, married, and the father of two daughters and a son, he lived with his family in Burlington, on the Iowa-Illinois border just west of Galesburg. Early in August 1866 Herndon reached him by mail, saying he needed information, not just about Ann but about life generally at New Salem. Soon there came a cordial, one-page reply, which incidentally bore the welcome news that Ann's mother still lived:

> I have the honor to acknowledge the receipt of your letter of 30th ult, making inquiry as to my knowledge of the early history of our martered president, which will require some time to answer intelligably, as I will have to consult our family record, my mother and elder brother, who are in Van Buren Co. Iowa. Any information I can give you I will take great pleasure in doing. I see some pretended histories of Mr. Lincoln's life which are manifestly in error in detail.
>
> I recall all the men named in your letter. If Row Herndon, Wm Green, Mentor Graham & John McNamar are living they will recollect me as the 3rd son of the family.

Encouraged, Herndon immediately wrote again, enclosing a list of questions and asking the favor of an early response. Robert's answer, dated August 12, renewed his assurance that, though he was "very much engrossed with business" and was in the process of moving from Burlington to Oskaloosa, he would try to have the answer ready by October 1, as Herndon asked:

> having been sent to this place at an early stage of the war as Provost Marshal of the 1st Congressional Dist. of Iowa, my residence here is temporary. When I get my answer I will if at all practicable visit you, as I would like a personal interview as there are some things involved in a full answer to your interrogatories of a delicate character.
>
> No charge for time, service or expense will be made, as I will be more than compensated if I can contribute anything to the history of that Great good man, whose name and fame will ever live green in the memory of a grateful American people.

The promised contribution, however, failed to reach Springfield by the first, and it was month's end before Robert wrote again. His reply was ready, he said, and only awaited copying: "I fully appreciate the importance of the answers to your questions, have compared notes with parties who were eyewitnesses to the incidents related." His planned visit to Springfield, he added, unfortunately would not take place because of the pressure of personal affairs.

Nervous over the delay, and with his lecture only two weeks off, Herndon now tried his luck with another of the Rutledges—he could hardly go before an audience to tell Ann's story without some measure of backing from her family. The reply he received from fifty-five-year-old John Rutledge of Birmingham, Iowa, was prompt but it was also disappointing. He preferred, said John, to leave matters to his brother: "Robert was here some time ago and we hunted up some papers and gave the information we could." That brief exchange virtually ended the direct involvement of John Rutledge in the project, a decided loss. A man of small education but intelligent and wise, he was a warm admirer of the young Lincoln and might, if pressed, have proved a major source of information. He ends his letter: "I was with him in the Black Hawk War, he was my Captain, a better man I think never lived on the earth."

A week before the lecture, Robert's lengthy answer to Herndon's "interrogatories" finally arrived at Springfield. While Herndon would have found it quite satisfactory for his own purposes, its value for study of the legend itself is less than might have been hoped. Fifteen pages in length, fewer than three of those pages talk of Abe and Ann, and little new is provided in the way of detail. Strangely, considering the source, Ohio rather than New York State is given as the place of McNamar's home. Apparently not only Robert but also his mother and brother, and perhaps others who should have known better, were still confusing the state of Ohio with the district of New York's Broome County known as New Ohio.

That Robert viewed his task seriously, framing his answers with extreme care, is shown by the letter's opening: "Believing that any authentic statements connected with the early life and history of the beloved Abraham Lincoln should belong to the great American people, I submit the following." A further remark sensibly gave Herndon some leeway, in fact full authority, in sifting and interpreting the information supplied. If he found "that the date, location, and circumstances of the events here named should be contradictory to those named from other sources," then he must "consider well," favoring that testimony which was least open to doubt. The section of the letter relating to Ann starts at the bottom of page 4 and runs through page 6, opening with an explanation of McNamar's role:

In 1830, my sister being then but seventeen years of age, a stranger calling himself John McNeil came to New Salem. He boarded with Mr. Cameron and was keeping a store with a Samuel Hill. A friendship grew up between McNeil and Ann which ripened apace and resulted in an engagement to marry. McNeil's real name was McNamar.

It seems that his father had failed in business, and his son, a very young man, had determined to make a fortune, pay off his father's debts, and restore him to his former social and financial standing. With this view he left his home clandestinely, and in order to avoid pursuit by his parents changed his name. His conduct was strictly high-toned, honest, and moral, and his object, whatever any may think of the deception which he practiced in changing his name, entirely praiseworthy.

He prospered in business and pending his engagement with

Ann, he revealed his true name, returned to Ohio to relieve his parents from their embarrassments, and to bring the family with him to Illinois. On his return to Ohio, several years having elapsed, he found his father in declining health or dead, and perhaps the circumstances of the family prevented his immediate return to New Salem. At all events he was absent two or three years.

Robert's failure to make more of McNamar's lengthy absence, or even to express any sort of curiosity over it, may argue that McNamar, on his return, finding Ann dead, never bothered with explanations. More to the point is what Robert had to say about Lincoln's entry into the picture, and the aftermath. With McNamar absent from New Salem, Lincoln began paying court to Ann—no mention is made of how long he waited after McNamar's departure. His frequent visits and attentions,

resulted in an engagement to marry, conditional to an honorable release from the contract with McNamar. There is no kind of doubt as to the existence of this engagement. David Rutledge urged Ann to consummate it, but she refused until such time as she could see McNamar, inform him of the change in her feelings, and seek an honorable release. Mr. Lincoln lived in the village, McNamar did not return, and in August 1835 Ann sickened and died. The effect upon Mr. Lincoln's mind was terrible; he became plunged in despair, and many of his friends feared that reason would desert her throne. His extraordinary emotions were regarded as strong evidence of the existence of the tenderest relations between himself and the deceased.

How Robert was able to describe so unblinkingly Lincoln's supposed terrible despair, yet offer no objective evidence or instances of it, forms an omission at least mildly puzzling. Surely his mother and brother, if not he himself, could have supplied the needed information, so historically relevant, from their own knowledge or by repeating what they had heard from others. Hurry or inattention perhaps may sufficiently explain the oversight, yet this question, too, probably ignores how matters actually stood at a period still so near the assassination. Not unreasonably, Robert may have felt that such grim personal exposure would not be proper while the shock of Lincoln's death was still reverberating. It was a day, after all, of strict reticence in such matters, especially so where the dignity of public figures was concerned.

Enclosed with his letter Robert sent a copy of a statement he had requested from another old neighbor, one who could supply firsthand knowledge of Lincoln's visits to the Rutledge home at Sandridge. John Jones, brother of Hannah Armstrong, Jack's wife, had served with Lincoln in the Black Hawk War and afterward had lived for years at Sandridge. Like so many others, he had then picked up and gone west, though not too far. His letter, dated October 22, 1866, from Winterset, Iowa, starts by giving full support to Robert's long letter to Herndon, which he says he has read. He goes on:

> As to the relation existing between Mr. Lincoln and Ann Rutledge, I have every reason to believe that it was of the tenderest character, as I know of my own knowledge that he made regular visits to her. During her last illness he visited her sick chamber and on his return stopped at my house. It was very evident that he was much distressed. I was not surprised when it was rumored subsequently that his reason was in danger. It was generally understood that Mr. Lincoln and Ann Rutledge were engaged to be married. She was a very amiable and lovable woman and it was deemed a very suitable match—one in which the parties were in every way worthy of each other.

One facet of this letter deserves to be highlighted in the roll call of evidence, for the two phrases relating to the engagement of the pair—"I have every reason to believe" and "It was generally understood"—when taken together may hold one of the keys to the legend. They seem to argue, and Jones seems to be implying, that Abe and Ann, while their intentions were pretty well known in the village, for some reason may never have officially made public their plans to marry.

This initial Rutledge testimony supplied the cap to Herndon's research regarding Ann, and when he stepped onto the platform of the Practical Business College in Springfield on the evening of November 16, 1866, he was much better prepared for his talk than has been imagined. The revelation he was to make that night, it seems, was based on at least a sufficiency of oral testimony, though perhaps not quite, as he would bravely claim, "in every particular."

In addition to eleven eyewitnesses, he had the blessings of Ann's family, most importantly including her mother. His files also held several other statements, though brief and offering little or no detail, from a half dozen more eyewitnesses, all pioneers of New Salem, all friends of the young Lincoln.[*] John Hill's *Axis* article added its own valuable support, for behind it lay Hill's own research among the old settlers, as well as the testimony of his father, a close friend of Lincoln at New Salem, and his mother, perhaps Ann's best friend. Such unanimous testimony coming from at least twenty knowledgeable witnesses, even where it took the form of anecdote, of reminiscence gathered long afterward, can scarcely be judged unimpressive. Thirty years is not really too long a period in which to hold, clear and undiminished, the memory of colorful and critical events. Where witnesses have remained close to the original site, have kept in touch with each other, and have passed the intervening years talking over how things were "back then," an astonishing amount of factual truth may be preserved.

ও

A last spurt of correspondence following the lecture closed out Herndon's dealings with the Rutledges. In some ways this later information proved every bit as valuable as all that had come before.

Three additional letters written in the last days of November arrived from Robert as follow-up comment on the portrait drawn by Herndon in his talk ("bold, manly, & substantially true," Robert thought the lecture). Excerpts from these not only add variety of detail to the legend, but they also somewhat expand its overall dimensions.

Two other New Salem suitors, Robert explained, had been involved with his sister, and she had rejected both before accepting McNamar. These were William Berry, who had been Lincoln's grocery store partner and who died the same year as Ann, and Samuel Hill, who married Parthena Nance only the month before Ann's death. It was some time after McNamar had left for his home in the East, Robert explained, that "Mr. Lincoln courted Ann, resulting in a second engagement, not conditional as my [earlier] language would seem to indicate, but absolute." The lovers had sensibly decided to delay the marriage, he added, until Lincoln had qualified as a lawyer.

On this facet of the legend Robert was able to offer further direct

---

[*]See chapter 7.

testimony, quoting from a recent letter he had received from his cousin McGrady Rutledge. "Ann told me once in coming from a Camp Meeting on Rock Creek", wrote McGrady, "that engagements made too far ahead sometimes failed, that one had failed, and gave me to understand that as soon as certain studies were completed she and Lincoln would be married." Concerning McGrady's cautious attitude, Robert comments: "He says you and Mr. Cogsdale [*sic*] talked much with him on this subject, but that he did not tell you much as he thot 'you had a design in it.' You can correspond with him and say to him that this is no longer a delicate subject." McGrady's suspicions, it may be, were linked somehow to Herndon's own politics.

According to Robert, one of Ann's other brothers, David, had tried to convince her that she bore no further obligation to the long-absent, long-silent McNamar, that she had every right to proceed to a wedding with Lincoln. But Ann had scrupulously insisted on "the propriety of seeing McNamar, informing him of the change in her feelings, & seeking an honorable release before consummating the engagement with Mr. L. by marriage."* But there was no doubt, Robert adds, that "Ann had fully determined to break off the engagement with McNamar." While he doesn't say so explicitly, his mother's agreement with that assertion may be taken for granted, as also that of his brothers and sisters, in particular John and Nancy.

As to Lincoln's mental sufferings on Ann's death, Robert's further comment at first seems a bit confusing with its claim of ignorance. "I cannot answer this question from personal knowledge," he writes, "but from what I have learned from others at the time, you are substantially correct." However, Robert's dearth of information on this point is also quite reasonable: "I cannot say whether Mr. Lincoln was radically a changed man after the event of which you speak [Ann's death] or not, as I saw little of him after that time." He adds that the cause of his sister's death was not emotional conflict, as Herndon thought, it was "brain fever."

Disappointingly, McGrady Rutledge faded rather rapidly from the picture, there being no record of any direct correspondence with him. Several statements he made much later, however, brief and incidental as they are, prove valuable as showing once again that it was Ann's

---

*The word "seeing" in this context may seem to ring false, since no one, supposedly, could tell when McNamar might return. But "seeing" is probably correct, as chapter 9 attempts to show.

personality (interestingly, in many ways like Lincoln's own), her air of
quiet joy in particular, that people remembered best:

> She was a beautiful girl, and as bright as she was pretty. She was
> well educated for that early day, a good conversationalist, and
> always gentle & cheerful; a girl whose company people liked....
> Everybody was happy with Ann. She was of a cheerful disposition,
> seeming to enjoy life, and helping others to enjoy it.

Toward the close of his life—he lived until 1899—McGrady penned a
short memoir of his days in Illinois, full of nostalgic recollections of
ordinary things. Its only reference to Lincoln occurs at the end, where
the thought leaps nimbly over a gap of more than sixty years:

> I had the honor to voat twice for the greatest man that ever lived,
> Abraham Lincoln. I had a long aquaintance with him. Him and I
> slept in the same bed while he boarded [at the tavern] with my
> uncle James Rutledge. While he was boarding there Lincoln became
> deeply in love with Ann. She was my cousin. Had she lived till
> spring they were to be married. Ann took sick, died August 25,
> 1835. Lincoln took her death verry hard.

By any measure, the evidence given by Ann's family, impressive by
virtue of its restraint and its sober tone, deserves serious attention. To
it may now be added still another Rutledge voice, one that has so far
been overlooked but which speaks convincingly. Affording a fresh view,
a new angle of approach, it derives from a Lincoln researcher who, like
John Hill, preceded Herndon.

The eldest Rutledge child was a girl named Jean. At Ann's death she
was twenty-six and had been married for six years. She herself was to
die somewhat prematurely in August 1866, just as Herndon was opening his contact with Robert. Some time before that—it may well have
been while Lincoln lived—a local historian spoke with Jean about old
New Salem days, recording her reply in his diary. The historian, R. D.
Miller of Springfield, about 1890 showed his diary to Ida Tarbell,
permitting her to quote from it. In these quoted passages—set down by
Miller in his diary perhaps as many as five years before Herndon
revealed Ann's story to the world, a fact of which Tarbell seems
unaware—Jean Rutledge, by then Mrs. James Berry, fully confirms her

sister's engagement to Lincoln. Ann's "whole soul seemed wrapped up" in him, she states, explaining that the two planned to marry in the fall of 1836, when Ann would have completed her proposed year of schooling. On Lincoln, Ann's sudden death exerted a profound effect, she added, leaving him woefully shaken:

> After Ann died I remember that it was common talk about how sad Lincoln was; and I remember myself how sad he looked. They told me that every time he was in the neighborhood after she died, he would go alone to her grave & sit there in silence for hours.*

That Jean actually told Miller a good deal more than that can be seen in a remark that occurs in Miller's own volume of local history, published in 1905 (revised from the 1879 edition). Jean, he says, supplied him with "many facts" concerning the romance of Abe and Ann "that are interesting in themselves and go to establish the truth of the affection between him and Miss Rutledge but are not of sufficient importance to be repeated here." With that exasperating sentence Miller dropped the subject. He never published anything further about his interview with Jean, and the location of his diary, if it survives, is unknown.

The last Rutledge to speak for the record was the reticent John. Second oldest in the family, he was twenty-five at Ann's death, so while he quotes his mother, he obviously had his own memories of that sad event. Almost casually he throws a sudden flash of light on his sister's final days, confirming the suspicion that he would have proved a fount of information. Late in November 1866 he wrote Herndon of his very real pleasure with the lecture, a copy of which had been sent him earlier. In what he says of Ann there may be detected a special poignance:

> With much embarism I attempt to answer from the fact I have no learning of any consequence. Should have done this some time ago but I have been very busy getting in my corn and am not well at present. . . . The lecture I am well pleased with, a part

---

*The phrase "they told me" is explained by the fact that Jean was married at the time Ann died and lived at Rock Creek, some miles south of the Rutledge home at Sandridge.

of it was read with a full heart to have the past years brought
fresh to memory. I often herd Mother say that the last time she
herd Annie sing was a few days before she was taken sick upstairs
in that old house of McNamar's like this,
   Vain man thy fond persuits forbare
   Repent thy end is nigh
   Death at the farthest cant be far.
   O think before thou dye, etc.
But I must close for I feel more like saying to myself, O my soul
when shall I be delivered from this body of clay. If I have said
anything wrong I hope to be corrected.

A distant echo of the Rutledges, occurring fully seven decades later,
was also struck through John. A great-granddaughter of his, also named
Ann Rutledge and looking like everyone's idea of the charming original,
made news in 1938 when she took the New York stage in a play about
Lincoln at New Salem, *Prologue to Glory.* Acting the role of her
by-then renowned great-grandaunt, she scored a decided hit.

7

A Parade of Witnesses

THE INSISTENT voices of nine more witnesses offering forthright comment on Ann Rutledge, all recorded by Herndon, throng to be heard. While this testimony has its own high value, less can be told of the people themselves and of their acquaintance with Lincoln, so each need be allowed on stage for no more than a cameo appearance. Five of the nine are old residents of New Salem and vicinity, and four are knowledgeable friends and relatives of eyewitnesses.

Added to this quick parade are observations by two people who knew Abe and Ann but whose memories, eminently worthy to be heard, were not set down until long afterward. A final witness, Joshua Speed, always identified as the mature Lincoln's best friend, supplies testimony that carries a special and rather peculiar, if problematic, relevance, and is considered separately. How much credence should be allowed any of the dozen is a question to be decided strictly within the framework of the information already presented.

I

Lynn McNulty ("Nult") Green, younger brother of William, wrote to Herndon in July 1865, one of the first to respond. Apologizing for the "paucity of information" he had to offer, he explains that for most of the time Lincoln lived at New Salem, "I was away from home at school excepting vacations." Green was also one of four New Salemites who claimed to have aided Lincoln in his study of Kirkham's grammar, which is entirely possible (the others were his brother Billy, Mentor

Graham, and Jason Duncan). Nult's stab at dating the engagement is wrong, much too early: "In the summer of 1833 he engaged to be married to Miss Ann Rutledge of New Salem a beautiful and very amiable young woman. But before the match was consummated she took fever and died. Lincoln took it very hard indeed." Green may have been still at home late that August when Ann died, or he may have already gone back to school. It is impossible to know.

2

George Spears of Clary's Grove, whose family was among the area's earliest settlers and whose mother was long active as a midwife, once nettled postmaster Lincoln by requesting a receipt for payment. The postage on his newspaper subscription was long overdue when Lincoln, jealous of his reputation for strict dealing, wrote him: "Now that I have waited a full year you choose to wound my feelings by insinuating that unless you get a receipt I will probably make you pay it again." No bad feelings resulted, and Spears later said that he had "seen enough in the first settling of New Salem & the early history of Mr. Lincoln's life if I had made notes of it to have filled a large volume."

In November 1866 Spears received from Herndon a copy of the Rutledge lecture. His brief comment was: "I read it carefully over & there is nothing in it but what is strictly true your description of New Salem is as correct as can be given, as to Mr. Lincoln's crazy spell I do not recollect."

3

Caleb Carman, originally of Sangamo Town, was a comparative latecomer to New Salem, arriving in 1833. Among other things, he was for a time associated with the Bale family in the wool carding business, and he later claimed that Lincoln was once a boarder at his house (since Lincoln took board at a half dozen cabins in the village, including lodging after he lost his store in 1833, there is no particular reason to doubt Carman's word on this). Interviewed by Herndon at Petersburg in October 1866, his lengthy reply (ten pages of handwritten notes) included only a brief mention of Ann: "He frequently visited from 1833 to 1837 young ladies—he courted Miss Rutledge: she moved down the river a few miles before Abe got to Salem. . . . Miss Rutledge was a pretty woman—good-natured—kind." The move "down the river" accurately recalls the Rutledges leaving New Salem for

Sandridge, but the move actually took place a year and a half *after* Lincoln's arrival in the village.

In addition, a letter Carman wrote Herndon a few weeks later has this: "You wished to know something about Lincoln's love with Ann Rutledge this I cannot tell much about it is true that he loved Miss Rutledge I suppose this happened before I came to New Salem." That Carman did not really know much about the romance, or the circumstances of the tragedy, seems evident from another statement in the same letter: "You wished to know something about the time Ann Rutledge died I cannot find out the time yet but will try."

4

Jason Duncan was a physician practicing in the New Salem area. He boarded at one time with Bowling Green, and he recalled how Lincoln's welcome visits to that house often sparked dryly humorous exchanges with the rotund, rollicking Green: "many were the laconic remarks made by these gentlemen to the amusement of any neighbor or friend who might happen to be present." Duncan's testimony about Ann, given in a letter of 1867, is important for another reason, for it helps to date the time of the engagement:

> He was very reserved toward the opposite sex. While I lived and boarded in the same place with him, do not recall of his ever paying his addresses to any young lady, though I knew he had great partiality for Miss Ann Rutledge. But at that time there was an insurmountable barrier in the way of his ambition, for her hand I have reason to know was promised to a man by the name of McNamar, or as he called himself at the time McNeil. The man left that part of the country and remained away for the space of a year or two I think without anyone knowing where he was. Most of the inhabitants supposed he never would return and [he] never did until after I left that part of the country which was in the autumn of 1834.

When Duncan moved northwest in the fall of 1834 to the town of Warsaw, Illinois, on the banks of the Mississippi, what he called the "barrier" of Ann's promise to McNamar still existed, or so he understood when looking back. The curious thing is that, even living at a distance as he was, he did later hear of McNamar's belated return, yet he apparently never heard of Ann's acceptance of Lincoln.

5

Henry Hohimer, then of Petersburg, formerly of Rock Creek and New Salem, where he was acquainted with Lincoln, in 1887 gave an interview to William Herndon. The reference to Ann, among the shortest Herndon collected, is also among the most tantalizing, and it is hard to see how Herndon could have let his man get away without pressing him for details. Said Hohimer: "Knew Lincoln well—knew Ann Rutledge well—handsome woman—it is my opinion that they were engaged—would have been married had she lived." On the same page there is another detached sentence linked to Hohimer, lone and unexplained: "Lincoln cut out McNamar."

6

B. F. Irwin, of Pleasant Plains, a village just south of Petersburg, himself an old resident of the area, did some investigating for Herndon in the summer of 1866. He succeeded in uncovering a few valuable facts, but he also created some initial confusion. His first statement was sent in August:

> In 1832 or 3 Lincoln was woefully in love with a remarkably handsome young lady by the name of Rutledge. 2 other men was in the same fix all thru paying their addresses to her—who was first in her estimation I know not. In the meantime she died and Lincoln took it so hard that some of his friends really thought that he would go crazy or was partially so about it.... I could give you the names of the two gentlemen after the young lady but that you dont wish or desire.

A month later Irwin wrote a second report. His uncertainty over Ann, whether then living or dead, probably stems from his own misinterpretation of what he had heard, especially from Isaac Cogdal (Ann's *family* was living in Iowa in 1860). Herndon, who had other sources better informed, by this time knew very well that Ann had died long before:

> In regard to Miss Rutledge, this I learn to be true. Lincoln, Samuel Hill (now deceased) and one McNamar was all paying

their respects to her at the same time. She did not seem to be very favorably impressed with Lincoln, at least so he thought. Lincoln was then young poor and awkward, the other two was up in the world. She married neither of the men, in addition she was very handsome, so considered at the time. My informants differ as to her death—one who pretends to know says she died but Cogdal says she was living in Iowa in 1860 as Lincoln told him.... There is two of the Rutledges still in or near Petersburg that is relations of the woman to wit Wm and McGrady Rutledge. They can tell if she is living still or died as Combs thinks in 1834. I do not know the men in person but know they are there. McNamar I also learn still lives in Menard County.

His various "informants" Irwin never named, nor did he state where he found them. The Combs mentioned was Jonah Combs, whom Irwin identifies in his first report as an "old personal and political friend" of Lincoln, but who is otherwise unidentified.

7

William McNeely, of Petersburg, was the son of Robert McNeely, an old New Salem man. Much fascinated by everything connected with his family's pioneer days, he went around in November 1866 at Herndon's request interviewing his father's old friends, with some interesting results:

I have talked with Bennett & other men who became acquainted with Mr Lincoln and lived near Salem shortly after the period of his reported *insanity*. They say that they learned from the people— the immediate associates and friends of Mr Lincoln—that he had been *insane,* that his mind had been *shaken*—that disappointed love was the cause—her name Miss Rutledge. It was then talked of as a part of the history of the men of the town. The extent of his insanity was such that men were *then* occassionally talking of it & it is *still* remembered by them.

Lincoln, old Maj. Hill & McNamar were in love with the girl. She died and Lincoln for sometime after so acted that everybody who knew and saw him pronounced him *crazy,* as they called it.... Father asks me to say that he never was in Lincoln's house.

On reading Herndon's lecture on Ann, McNeely wrote him that he had correctly described Lincoln's condition, "except when you say that the 'mental dethronement of his reason could only be detected by his closest friends.' He may not have been for a time totally insane but he was so near that condition that everybody who saw and knew him at once set him down as insane." This offhand remark actually provides another clue to the truth of Lincoln's state of mind at the time. It was not the condition itself but the *contrast* that so forcibly struck his friends, the stark and sudden difference to be observed between Lincoln's usual bright manner, talkative and cheerful, and the silent, darkly ponderous gloom that enveloped him at Ann's death. Added to this extreme mood swing was his sustained desire for solitude, so unlike him, and his lone visits to Ann's grave. No wonder some of those earthy-minded pioneers, not given to subtlety in their judgments, thought him "insane" (a word that for them may have meant something less than actual derangement).

8

William Bennett, of Petersburg, son and nephew of the Bennett brothers, who were among the town's original settlers, spoke with Herndon in the fall of 1866. Only a brief note of what he said has survived: "Heard a conversation among the older settlers—such as Squire Short—Godbey & others and it was their opinion that Lincoln and Ann Rutledge were engaged to be married."

The Squire mentioned was the same Uncle Jimmy Short who rescued Lincoln's surveying instruments and who in an earlier letter to Herndon said he was unaware of any engagement or "tender passages" between Abe and Ann. Russell Godbey was a New Salemite for whom Lincoln in the spring of 1834 did one of his first surveying jobs. He achieved a permanent place in Lincoln lore when in later years he told the story on himself about finding young Abe at midday stretched atop a village woodpile holding a book. Silently wondering why the strapping young man wasn't doing some useful work, Godbey asked what he was reading. Not reading, said Abe, I'm studying. What was he studying? Law, was the reply. "Good God A'mighty!" commented Godbey as he strode off.

9

Lizzie Bell, daughter of Mentor Graham, was born in 1833 at her father's house a half mile outside New Salem. Too young to have retained any clear memory of the incidents of village life, what she told Herndon at an 1887 interview came from memories of her parents' talk over the years and from her friendships with New Salem women, particularly the Bale girls. Herndon's scurrying notes with their fragmentary air, probably do not record all that Mrs. Bell told him. Obviously wrong is her reference to Samuel Hill, for Ann had rejected his suit before accepting McNamar:

Fanny Bale had a quilting at the request of Lincoln in New Salem—Ann Rutledge was there—Ann I think had her eye on Hill more than on Lincoln—dont think that Ann Rutledge was absolutely engaged to Lincoln though she sent for him during her last sickness. At the quilting Fanny had her eye on Lincoln and Lincoln had his eye on Ann—to make Ann a little more attentive to Lincoln he L seemed to go for Miss Bale. Miss B. stuck a needle in her finger—Lincoln pulled it out—Lincoln quilted on the quilt a time or two. The quilt is [two words illegible]. Lincoln's acts nettled Ann to a kind of [one word illegible]. Ann paid him back in his own coin. Lincoln would ask my mother if he should marry this or that woman. Lincoln & Ann had a fly-up, but on her death bid them send for Lincoln & all things were reconciled.

10

Harvey Ross as a young man carried the U.S. mails on the route between Springfield and Lewistown, passing through New Salem four times a week, twice out and twice back. "I would often assist Mr. Lincoln in his store," he recalled, "and in sorting over the mail, and he would often send packages by me to his customers along the road." Sometimes Ross stopped overnight at the Rutledge tavern where he got to know Ann (this would refer to the period before early summer 1833, when Ann went north to join her parents on the farm at Sandridge):

She was two or three years younger than Lincoln, of about medium size, weighing 125 pounds. She was very handsome and attractive, as well as industrious and sweet-spirited. I seldom saw her when she was not engaged in some occupation—knitting, sewing, waiting on table, etc. I think she did the sewing for the entire family.

Ross's account of Lincoln's early years was included in his book *Early Pioneers and Pioneer Events of Illinois,* which is obviously colored by his reading in other printed sources. Even so, what he says about Lincoln and Ann should not be ignored, for he was frequently in Lincoln's presence during the critical years 1834–35, with unusual chances for observation. The curious thing about his description of the romance is the absence of any mention of John McNamar:

At this time Lincoln boarded at the Rutledge tavern, at which I also put up as often as I went to New Salem. It was a hewed log house, two stories high, with four rooms above and four below. It had two chimneys with large fireplaces, and not a stove in the house. The proprietor was James Rutledge, a man of more than ordinary ability, and, with his wife, remarkably kind and hospitable. They had a large family of eight or nine children, and among them was their daughter Anne. . . .

Lincoln was boarding at the tavern and fell deeply in love with Anne, and she was no less in love with him. They were engaged to be married, but they had been putting off the wedding for a while, as he wanted to accumulate a little more property, and she wanted to go longer to school.

Before the time came when they were to be married, Miss Anne was taken down with typhoid fever and lay desperately ill four weeks. Lincoln was an anxious and constant watcher at her bedside. The sickness ended in her death, and young Lincoln was heartbroken and prostrate. The histories have not exaggerated his pitiful grief. For many days he was not able to attend to business. . . . His friends did everything that kindness could suggest, but in vain, to soothe his sorrow.

So much, Ross might have attained on his own. The few added details he gives are by now familiar and were clearly picked up from other works.

II

Arminda Rogers Rankin, of Athens, a village just to the east of New Salem, put her personal recollections of her friend Ann on record through her son Henry. Ten years older than Ann, and with some experience as a teacher, Arminda "tutored the young girl in Blair's *Rhetoric,* Kirkham's *Grammar,* and the elementary studies she was reviewing" for entrance to the academy at Jacksonville. It is noticeable that the passage quoted below, while fixing the date of Ann's studies with Mrs. Rankin in the first half of 1835, nearly up to the onset of Ann's illness, makes no specific mention of an engagement:

As to how the engagement of Miss Rutledge to Lincoln came about, or how long after McNamar's absence and his neglect in writing to her, my mother's knowledge was indefinite. She said that in the latter part of 1834, when she saw the two young people together, there was an increasing interest between them. This increased from time to time so that it was apparent to her that Miss Rutledge was passing out of and above the depression and anxiety she had shown over McNamar's absence and neglect, and that there was a new love coming into her life.... My mother said she was not told by the young girl, at first, of this decision and of her acceptance of Lincoln, but that she felt assured of it by the increasing interest she took in her studies through the spring and summer of 1835, and by the buoyancy of her spirits as she talked about going to Jacksonville.... In the early summer, having finished the studies through which my mother had tutored her, she then fully confided to mother the secret of the new light that had come into her life.

Of still further interest in connection with the large, well-educated Rogers family is the fact, apparently well attested, that Lincoln himself was quite friendly with them. He borrowed books of Arminda's father, Col. Matthew Rogers, who was postmaster of Athens, and probably received help from the daughter with his own studies. This close personal link of Arminda with Abe and Ann in the crucial year 1835 makes her witness specially valuable (present-day historians' low opinion of her son Henry's reminiscences—he was once a student in the Lincoln law office—need not cancel or diminish what he gives as from his mother). Since she lived until 1892, it is a wonder how Herndon could have so completely missed consulting with her and with other members of the family.*

12

Joshua Speed, of Springfield and Louisville, responded to Herndon's Rutledge lecture two weeks after it was delivered. Though he had been Lincoln's most intimate friend, it appears that Lincoln never told him anything about Ann (the two first met some six months after her death but did not become well acquainted for another year). Apparently, also, he never heard the story elsewhere. One phrase in his letter responding to Herndon's inquiry has always been gratefully quoted by opponents of the legend—"It is all new to me"—an admission that definitely requires pondering. Yet quite a different impression is gained, dissipating much of the doubt, if more of the letter is read. Though he never heard of Ann, Speed shows himself in no way reluctant to credit Herndon's discovery: "I thank you for your last lecture. It is all new to me. But so true to my appreciation of Lincoln's character that independent of my knowledge of you I would almost swear to it." Evidently, what Speed is willing to "swear to" is not just the existence of Ann but also the claim in the lecture about the devastating effect on Lincoln of her death. That meaning is rather plain even on the letter's surface, but it has so far been ignored by doubters.

The information Speed volunteers next, about Lincoln consulting a doctor, added still another inviting line of inquiry to the legend. Unfortunately, it seems now beyond the possibility of pursuit:

> Lincoln wrote a letter (a long one which he read to me) to Dr. Drake of Cincinati descriptive of his case. Its date would be in Decr 40 or early in January 41. I think that he must have informed Dr. D. of his early love for Miss Rutledge, as there was a part of the letter which he would not read. It would be worth much to you if you could procure the original. Chas. Drake of St. Louis may have his father's papers. The date which I give you will aid in the search. I remember Dr. Drake's reply, which was that he would not undertake to prescribe for him without a

---

*For further on the link between Lincoln, Ann, and Arminda Rogers, see pp. 127–28.

personal interview. I would advise you to make some effort to get the letter.

The reference to Dr. Drake, of course, connects with Lincoln's later troubled courtship of Mary Todd during 1840–41, a much-embroiled topic and one thankfully beyond the scope of the present work. But perhaps this much by way of commentary on the letter may find agreement: Speed, who knew all there was to know about the broken engagement between Lincoln and his future wife, readily accepts the idea—indeed himself proposes it—that the memory of the dead Ann might somehow have played its own emotionally disruptive part in what happened. He may have been wrong—the unread portion of Lincoln's letter may not have concerned Ann at all or may have concerned her only in some innocuous fashion. But his willingness to believe that Ann's name did come up in Lincoln's letter to Drake, and not just in passing, deserves to be accorded its proper place in the legend.

One further item in this regard, seldom if ever noted, is the interesting coincidence between Speed's memory and a link at this same time to another doctor, this one in Springfield. On January 20, 1841, some three weeks after the breaking of the engagement with Mary Todd, Lincoln in a letter urged J. T. Stuart, then in Congress, to arrange a local government appointment for Dr. Anson Henry, then and later to be a close friend of both Lincolns. "You know I desired Dr. Henry to have that place when you left," wrote Lincoln. "I now desire it more than ever. I have, within the last few days, been making a most discreditable exhibition of myself in the way of hypochondriaism and thereby got an impression that Dr. Henry is necessary to my existence. Unless he gets the place he leaves Springfield. You therefore see how much I am interested in the matter. . . . My heart is verry much set upon it." This intense and open concern with having a trusted physician readily available to him serves at least to support Speed's own undocumented recollection.

Daniel Drake, M.D., originally of Cincinnati, later of Louisville, died at age sixty-seven in 1852. A very widely known figure of the time, author of medical texts and professor at the famous Louisville Medical Institute, he was a leader in the advance of nineteenth-century medicine. Despite Speed's urging Herndon to follow up on the clue (he was right about Drake's son Charles having the papers), Lincoln's letter has never been traced. How or why Lincoln was led to consult him in the first place, and by mail, has yet to be determined. Just possibly, the suggestion may have come from Dr. Henry. Part of Henry's medical education was received at Drake's well-known medical school in Cincinnati, and in any case he would certainly have known of him by reputation.

Years later, Dr. Henry was to assert in a letter that Lincoln "told me things which he says he has never yet named to anybody else." Whether those "things" referred also to earlier days, and included a mention of Ann Rutledge, is at present unknowable. If Henry had not died suddenly in the summer of 1865—he was drowned in a shipwreck off the California coast—he might have left more on record.

8

The Matter of Mary Owens

ANN RUTLEDGE had been at rest in Concord Cemetery little more than a year when the man whose shattered heart had supposedly been buried with her suddenly turned to another woman, this one very much alive. Also first uncovered by William Herndon, Lincoln's long-known and undoubted romance with Mary Owens has served to convince many that the picture of his consuming sorrow over the loss of Ann has been very far overdrawn. A second love affair, it is charged, one so speedily commenced, does not argue well for the existence of prior heartbreak or undying devotion to the first. While not in itself decisive, as it is presently understood the Mary Owens interlude does indeed pose a definite obstacle for upholders of the legend. It is also true, however, that the Owens story, like that of Ann, has never yet been seen in a proper light. Rather than negating the legend, under close scrutiny it yields surprising confirmation.

Even before Lincoln began his courtship of Ann, Mary Owens had made a brief entry into his life. The well-bred daughter of a wealthy Kentucky landowner, she came to New Salem in the fall of 1833 to visit her sister Elizabeth, wife of the prosperous Dr. Bennett Abell. Lincoln by then had become a warm friend of the Abells, frequently calling at their home just to the north of the village. "My little cabin on the hill," Mrs. Abell later styled the house, her nostalgia obscuring the fact that she and her husband had owned one of the area's finest farms. There and at other homes in the vicinity (Mary had blood ties to several other residents, including the Greens and Mentor Graham),

Lincoln several times encountered her during the month of her stay. Just concluding as she arrived was the first full year of John McNamar's absence, but whether Lincoln had begun so early to think of Ann as once more ripe for courting is doubtful—the probability is that he had not. In any case, all that is known of Lincoln's reaction to Mary at this juncture is contained in his own later admission that in 1833 he had found her "intelligent and agreeable."

A year older than Lincoln, Mary in appearance was the opposite of the fragile Ann but with a certain distinction of her own. She stood five feet five inches tall and weighed, by her own estimate, "about one hundred fifty pounds," though some in the village added another ten pounds and an inch or two to those figures. With dark, curling hair, fair skin, and eyes of deep blue, she was not thought of as pretty but rather as striking. Esther Bale said later that Mary was "handsome, that is to say, noble-looking, matronly seeming," a description echoed by others including Lincoln, who said he had never met a woman with a "finer face." Well educated, she was an easy talker with a friendly manner and a ready wit.

Three years after her first visit, some fourteen months after Ann's death, Mary arrived back at New Salem, this time prepared to stay. She had come at the invitation of her sister, Mrs. Abell, who had assumed the role of matchmaker. Pleasantly recalling each other from their first meetings, at the urging of Mrs. Abell Lincoln and Mary had agreed to consider marriage if further acquaintance confirmed the attraction.* Nothing specific of Mary's own view of the plan, aside from her agreement to it, has survived. Lincoln later confessed that he found himself "confoundedly well pleased" by the suggestion.

Between Mary's second arrival in New Salem, on November 7, 1836, and Lincoln's impending departure for Vandalia to take up his duties in the Illinois legislature lay a period of only three weeks. Since he would be gone from New Salem for nearly three months, the timing of Mary's visit for so delicate a purpose was not well managed, to say the least. As it turned out, however, it suited Lincoln very well, for no sooner had the two met again than he decided, as he said later, that he was "not at all pleased" by what he saw. Mary now struck him as

---

*The exact arrangement is difficult to pin down. It perhaps should be expressed as: had actually agreed to marry, barring some unforeseen impediment. Quick and rather casually arranged marriages, of course, were not uncommon on the frontier.

being decidedly unattractive, much heavier and older than he remembered her, perhaps duller, defects for which her intelligence and her cultured personality no longer seemed to compensate. That she also had to bear comparison in Lincoln's memory with the dainty, charming Ann could not have helped.

Still, feeling that he was to some extent obligated, prizing honor above all else, he tried to reason himself into a more acquiescent frame of mind. To himself, he emphasized Mary's noble appearance and warm nature, and he argued that intellect counted for more than "the person." But he was not quite convinced. While he dutifully studied how he might, as he expressed it, "get along through life after my contemplated change of circumstances," he also began fiercely calculating "how I might procrastinate the evil day."

His first letter to Mary, from Vandalia, was not written until two weeks after his arrival there, and then he talked mostly about politics, offering no endearments but showing himself to be fretful and depressed. He had fallen sick soon after his arrival, he wrote, and that fact "with other things I cannot account for, have conspired and have gotten my spirits so low, that I feel I would rather be any place in the world than here." Mary's letters to him (none have survived), according to what he said himself, showed that she had caught no hint of the real reason for his low spirits. Toward the idea of marriage with Lincoln, during the three months of his absence, she continued well disposed.

By early March 1837 Lincoln was back in New Salem, but now there came another interruption of at least a week, during which he handled some court cases in Springfield, marking his formal debut as a lawyer in partnership with John Stuart. Then in mid-April he made his final move from New Salem—planned long since, his going apparently had no connection with Mary's presence—taking up permanent residence in Springfield. With all his belongings stuffed into a saddlebag, he left New Salem village on horseback, and it was three weeks before he was ready again to write Mary, still staying with her sister. The prospect of marriage, it seems, was as much alive as ever. Yet it would have been strange had the astute Mary failed to sense the strong current of doubt under Lincoln's solicitous words:

Friend Mary,

I have commenced two letters to send you before this, both of which displeased me before I got half done, and so I tore them up. The first I thought wasn't serious enough, and the second was on the other extreme. I shall send this, turn out as it may—

This thing of living in Springfield is rather a dull business after all, at least it is so to me. I am quite as lonesome here as I ever was anywhere in my life. I have been spoken to by but one woman since I've been here, and should not have been by her, if she could have avoided it. I've never been to church yet, nor probably shall not be soon. I stay away because I am conscious that I should not know how to behave myself—

I am often thinking about what we said of your coming to live at Springfield. I am afraid you would not be satisfied. There is a great deal of flourishing about in carriages here; which it would be your doom to see without sharing in it. You would have to be poor without the means of hiding your poverty. Do you believe you could bear that patiently? Whatever woman may cast her lot with mine, should any ever do so, it is my intention to do all in my power to make her happy and contented; and there is nothing I can imagine that would make me more unhappy than to fail in the effort. I know I should be much happier with you than the way I am, provided I saw no signs of discontent in you. What you have said to me may have been in jest, or I may have misunderstood it. If so, then let it be forgotten; if otherwise, I much wish you would think seriously before you decide. For my part, I have already decided. What I have said I will most positively abide by, provided you wish it. My opinion is, that you had better not do it. You have not been accustomed to hardship, and it may be more severe than you now imagine.

I know you are capable of thinking correctly on any subject, and if you deliberate maturely upon this, before you decide, then I am willing to abide your decision.

Revealingly, whether consciously or not, in the weeks or months following, Lincoln can be glimpsed reinforcing by his personal behavior the uncertainties rather glaringly hinted at in the letter. Two incidents are recorded— small enough, yet thoroughly untypical of Lincoln, and to that extent pertinent—that show him being crudely thoughtless, acting somewhat the boor, in Mary's company.

The first incident concerns a long uphill walk in which he and Mary were accompanied by Nancy Green, who with her husband the year before had taken such loving care of the stricken Lincoln. On this walk—from the Green cabin at the foot of the hill to the Abell place at the summit, a distance of about a half mile—Mrs. Green was laboring under the burden of a large, heavy child. Lincoln, strolling along with the two women, made no move to take the child but kept up a stream of banter, the obvious omission considerably nettling Mary, as she later confessed. The second incident was more blatant. A company of young people from the village were out horseback riding, and the party came to a shallow, rock-strewn creek in which the footing looked treacherous. All the men guided their companions' horses across, but not Lincoln, who conspicuously rode on ahead, leaving Mary to herself. When she caught up with him and complained mildly of the neglect, he laughed and replied flippantly that he guessed she was "plenty smart to take care of" herself. Recalling the scene for Herndon, Mary said she supposed the remark was made "by way of compliment," which she perhaps believed.

For the relations of the two during the remainder of the year 1837 there survives only a single document, another letter of Lincoln's to Mary, but it is enough. One of the cleverest, most deliberately crafted letters he ever wrote—for balanced subtlety it is hardly surpassed by any of his political speeches or wartime communiqués—it was clearly fashioned with one object in mind, that of inducing Mary to reject his formal proposal of marriage. As Lincoln saw it by then, his only means of honorable escape from his predicament would be Mary's own freely chosen, outright refusal to marry him. This letter, it is herewith confidently suggested, was a last desperate attempt to bring that about. The two had met on August 16, either at Springfield or New Salem, and had spent a disquieting day together:

Friend Mary,

You will, no doubt, think it rather strange that I should write you a letter on the same day on which we parted; and I can only account for it by supposing, that seeing you lately makes me think of you more than usual, while at our late meeting we had but few expressions of thoughts. You must know that I cannot see you, or think of you, with entire indifference; and yet it may be that you are mistaken in regard to what my real feelings toward you are. If I knew you were not, I should not trouble you with this letter. Perhaps any other man would know enough

without further information; but I consider it *my* peculiar right to
plead ignorance, and your bounden duty to allow the plea.

I want in all cases to do right; and more particularly so in all
cases with women. I want, at this particular time, more than
anything else, to do right with you, and if I *knew* it would be
doing right, as I rather suspect it would, to let you alone, I would
do it. And for the purpose of making the matter as plain as
possible, I now say that you can now drop the subject, dismiss
your thoughts (if you ever had any) from me forever, and leave
this letter unanswered, without calling forth one accusing murmur from me. And I will go even further and say that if it will
add anything to your comfort, or peace of mind to do so, it is my
sincere wish that you should. Do not understand by this that I
wish to cut your acquaintance. I mean no such thing. What I do
wish is, that our further acquaintance shall depend upon yourself.
If such further acquaintance will contribute nothing to your
happiness, I am sure it would not to mine. If you feel yourself in
any degree bound to me, I am now willing to release you,
provided you wish it; while on the other hand I am willing and
even anxious to bind you faster, if I can be convinced that it will,
in any considerable degree, add to your happiness. This indeed is
the whole question with me. Nothing would make me more
miserable than to believe you miserable—nothing more happy
than to know you were so.

In what I have now said, I think I can not be misunderstood;
and to make myself understood, is the only object of this letter.

If it suits you best not to answer this, farewell—a long life and
a merry one attend you. But if you conclude to write back, speak
as plainly as I do. There can be neither harm nor danger in saying
to me anything you think, just in the manner you think it.

My respects to your sister.

Faced with this tortuous declaration, there are few women, certainly
not the sensitive and intelligent Mary Owens, who would or could
have accepted an offer of marriage from its author. Certain of the
letter's stark phrases would have put all the remainder—its overlay of
earnestness—in shadow. As he does "in all cases with women," he
explains almost briskly, he is eager to "do right with you," sober
words carrying at that day no more warmth or affection than they do

now. It might be the best thing, he suggests, if he were from that moment "to let you alone," and the idea takes on a feeling almost of urgency. Coming to the crux, he says that should *she* wish to break matters off, the move will bring from him no protest, not even "one accusing murmur" (almost too broad a hint!). At last he presents a veiled "sincere wish" that she *will* decide to end the affair, and in that case he is very "willing to release" her. When, some days or weeks later he did make his formal proposal, she turned him down. The offer he repeated several times at intervals, with each refusal becoming surer that he had gotten out of the "scrape," as he called it, without the slightest stain touching his "word, honor, or conscience."

By fall 1837 this particular strange encounter was finished, and early in the spring Mary departed from New Salem for the return to Kentucky. Years later she would tell Herndon that her refusal had been dictated by a simple matter of incompatability: "I thought Mr. Lincoln was deficient in those little links which make up the chain of woman's happiness—at least, it was so in my case. . . . his training had been different from mine; hence there was not that congeniality which would otherwise have existed." Despite his cruder background, if Lincoln had truly wished to impress Mary, he could not really have been ignorant of her watchful attitude toward "those little links." It is very probable, in fact, that there had been several other awkward or, say, vexing moments beyond the child-carrying and the creek-crossing, perhaps a whole series of them, to annoy the unsuspecting young woman.

So far as Mary Owens was concerned, that ended matters. For historians, on the other hand, there was an epilogue of sorts to deal with, since the vastly relieved Lincoln now chose to do a strangely uncharacteristic thing. While busy with politics at Vandalia he had made some new friends in the legislature, among them Senator Orville Browning and his wife. The youthful Eliza Browning, in particular, outgoing and sophisticated as she was, he found to be congenial. Soon he was writing her a lengthy and curiously jocular description of his recently concluded courtship, in the process producing a document that has disturbed, if not embarrassed, many readers since. He opens by explaining the matchmaking arrangement, then he mentions his first meeting with Mary and her subsequent return to the village as a prospective bride. He goes on:

although I had seen her before, she did not look as my imagination had pictured her—I knew she was oversize, but she now appeared a fair match for Falstaff; I knew she was called an "old maid," and I felt no doubt of the truth of at least half of the appelation; but now, when I beheld her, I could not for my life avoid thinking of my mother; and this, not from withered features, for her skin was too full of fat to permit its contracting into wrinkles; but from her want of teeth, weather-beaten appearance in general, and from a kind of notion that ran in my head that nothing could have commenced at the size of infancy, and reached her present bulk in less than thirty-five or forty years; and in short I was not at all pleased with her—But what could I do? I had told her sister that I would take her for better or for worse; and I made a point of honor and conscience in all things to stick to my word, especially if others had been induced to act on it, which in this case I doubted not they had, for I was now fairly convinced that no other man on earth would have her. . . .

Shortly after this, without attempting to come to any positive understanding with her, I set out for Vandalia, where and when you first saw me—During my stay there I had letters from her, which did not change my opinion of either her intellect or intention; but on the contrary, confirmed it in both—

All this while, although I was fixed "firm as the surge-repelling rock" in my resolution, I found I was continually repenting the rashness which had led me to make it—Through life I have been in no bondage, either real or imaginary, from the thralldom of which I so much desired to be free—

His extrication from the predicament he also records, but in tha now-famous passage he rings some changes, picturing Mary's refusal as taking him by surprise. His ingenious letter to her of August 16 he omits mentioning, and he puts a twist on the outcome of the affair that belies the real anquish he felt through it all:

I was mortified, it seemed to me, in a hundred different ways—My vanity was deeply wounded by the reflection that I had so long been too stupid to discover her intentions, and at the same time never doubting that I understood them perfectly; and also, that she whom I had taught myself to believe nobody else would have, had actually rejected me with all my fancied greatness; and to cap the whole, I then for the first time, began to suspect that I was really a little in love with her—But let it all go—I'll try and outlive it—Others have been made fools of by the girls, but this can never be with truth said of me—I most emphatically, in this instance, made a fool of myself—I have now come to the conclusion never again to think of marrying, and for this reason; I can never be satisfied with anyone who would be block-head enough to have me—

As more than one commentator has noted, only the facts that the letter was private, mentioned no names, sustained a jocular, self-deprecating note, and is dated April 1—all of which led the Brownings for years to think it an elaborate April Fool's joke dreamed up by their humorous friend—saves it from being a sadly unworthy production. This is correct and just, of course, though there are many who disagree, insisting that Lincoln's offense against taste, whatever its excuse, was blatant and should not be reasoned away. But in any case, it now can be said that there was a great deal more of significance involved than simple bad manners. In reality, the Browning letter marks one of the hitherto unguessed but truly historic turning points of Lincoln's early life: it identifies, while commemorating, the period in which he finally began to emerge from his grieving over Ann. This apparently light-hearted missive is nothing more or less than a veiled record of his recovery from the case of severe melancholia he had for many months silently endured. Mary Owens was the mechanism fate had provided toward that end.

The factor that links the two women, Mary and Ann, binding together the two love affairs and revealing their essential affinity, the one giving rise to the other, is the third woman in the curious venture, matchmaker Elizabeth Abell.

❧

Even in a society that took often inordinate pride in its hearty friendliness, the Abells were exceptional. William Herndon, who several times enjoyed what he called their "unbounded hospitality," remembered the doctor and his wife as an exceedingly warmhearted and generous pair, even styling them "jovial," as well as being lovers of company. Their house, he said, was always "wide open" to everyone, and they had the means to indulge themselves as hosts, for both had come of wealthy families back in Kentucky. In the isolated, rough-and-ready village of New Salem, the Abells "lived well and had all they wished."

Among those who were regular visitors at the Abell house, the talkative, companionable Lincoln was especially welcome (for him a good part of the attraction would have been the Abells' large stock of books, mostly on historical subjects). Whenever he was in the neighborhood, particularly on his surveying trips, he would be their overnight guest, and he was treated, according to what Mrs. Abell told Herndon, as one of the family:

> He was always social and lively...the best-natured man I ever got acquainted with. He stayed at our house on the bluff when he was surveying all those hills between us and Petersburg. Our oldest boy carried the [surveying] chain for him. Whenever he would come in at night all dragged [out] and scratched up with the bryers he would laugh over it and say that was a poor man's lot. I told him to get me a Buck Skin and I would fix him so the bryers would not scratch him—he done so and I foxed his pants for him [sewed protective buckskin on the legs].

During the trying period of Ann's fatal illness—its length is variously estimated at a week or two to a month or more—Lincoln would often stop at the Abell place while going to or returning from the Rutledge farm at Sandridge. Probably he was drawn to the Abells as much for the soothing effect of their sympathetic natures as for a night's rest. He was there when Ann died—on this Mrs. Abell's word may be accepted—staying with them for a few days after the funeral. The Abells thus become perhaps the most important witnesses of all to the true state of Lincoln's emotions at Ann's death, and it is fortunate that Mrs. Abell left even the little on record that she did. The following all-too-brief paragraph occurs in her letter of February 1867 to Herndon. Its implications suggest how much additional light she and her husband might have shed:

> The courtship between him and Miss Rutledge I can say but little, this much I do know he was staying with us at the time of her

death. It was a great shock to him and I never seen a man mourn more for a companion than he did for her. He made a remark one day when it was raining that he couldn't bare the idea of its raining on her Grave. That was the time when the community said he was crazy he was not crazy but he was very disponding a long time.

The letter ends with an invitation which shows that the writer was ready and willing, even eager, to say much more than she was able to put down on paper: "If I could see you I could tell you a great many things—I can talk better than I can write." Herndon, however, his energy and resources already faltering, by now had ended his researches and had begun to think of selling his documents to Lamon. He never went to see Mrs. Abell and the correspondence lapsed.

What information of value might Mrs. Abell have told Herndon about Abe and Ann? For one, by expanding on the claim that she had never seen a man "mourn more for a companion," perhaps supplying a day-by-day picture of Lincoln's behavior in his depression, she might have come near settling that still-vexed question, helping to fix its depth and duration. Just as important, perhaps more so, she could have sketched the Mary Owens interlude in all its completeness and complexity, including her own crucial part as go-between, and it is in this area that her exclusive testimony promised most. Herndon was aware of her blood relationship to Mary Owens. Had he questioned her he might well have caught the revealing link, rather obvious now, between Lincoln's continued deep depression of spirit and Mrs. Abell's urging him to think again of taking a wife.

"The community said he was crazy," wrote Mrs. Abell, adding firmly, "he was not crazy but he was very disponding a long time." Just *how* long, Herndon might have asked, and just *when* had the name Mary Owens first come up in the context of an arranged marriage? In the ordinary course, Mary's coming to New Salem would have been talked over with her sister some months *before* her arrival there in the fall of 1836. Lincoln's depression, to judge by the various witnesses and even at its shortest duration, would have clung to him for some months *after* Ann's death in the fall of 1835. With those two converging dates in mind, by posing a single question to Mrs. Abell, Herndon might have accomplished much: on the day when you made the suggestion to Lincoln about Mary Owens as a possible wife, what was his mood and manner? Did he still show signs of depression? To that imaginary inquiry, it is here suggested, Mrs. Abell would have answered candidly, giving a decided *yes*—and she might have gone on to assure her questioner of what was probably the truth, that she had made her move for that very reason. The compassionate Mrs. Abell would not have been the first to argue that a loving wife could work wonders and was just what the brooding Lincoln needed.

As a conclusion to the remarkable Owens episode, considering all that has been said and suggested, perhaps the following may be ventured without inviting wholesale contradiction.

Lincoln entered his marriage pact with Mary at a time when he was still suffering from the very real and potentially quite damaging effects of clinical melancholia, his perceptions all awry. Often misunderstood as a mere matter of dejection or of temporary depression of spirits, melancholia is actually a serious mental condition or disease, with specific causes and symptoms. Depending on the often unpredictable, always quicksilverish circumstances, it can lead to all sorts of abberant behavior, passive or active. In its milder form it may cause but little outward disruption of the daily routine, as it appears to have done with Lincoln. According to the sufferer's original temperament, in varying degrees the threat of actual insanity may arise, and even thoughts of suicide (Herndon was not entirely wrong, only imaginatively excessive, when he saw a good deal of Hamlet in his sorrowing friend). Finally, and also a recognized fact of melancholia, it was Lincoln's unthinking misstep with Mary that afforded him the very means—his sudden shocked realization of what he had done—by which he would begin to master his disability.

Not all at once, but gradually during the fall and winter of 1836–37, as he struggled to undo without causing further hurt a mistake that he knew would be a disaster for both parties, he came to himself. After more than a year of silent misery, perceiving a threat to the entire remainder of his life, Lincoln at last began to awake from his dream of despair over Ann.

9

His Heart in Her Grave?

ENTERING THE front door of Hill's general store on Main Street in New Salem, young Matthew Marsh was disappointed to find the postmaster absent. In Hill's store now—the fall of 1835—was housed the town post office, and Marsh was eagerly awaiting money from home, urgently needed to pay off a debt. A glance at the large cabinet that held the U.S. mails showed that its doors had been left open. Hesitating only a second, he began sifting through the piles of pigeonholed letters, soon spotting his name on one. To his relief, along with a letter from his parents in New Hampshire there was an order for one hundred dollars. Postage due on the letter was twenty-five cents, which the grateful Marsh no doubt left with a note in the cabinet.

Next day, September 17, Marsh began writing what became a very long answer to his parents, telling of his life in the frontier settlement. He actually spent several days on its composition, never dreaming that in his homey opening paragraph he was producing a document destined, when discovered some ninety years later, to take on a peculiar historical significance. The friend he mentions, Charles Clarke, also a New Salem resident, had been back East for a visit and his return was overdue (Clarke showed up ten days later, having been a full month on his journey by land and water):

Dear Folks:

I have received your letters of July 21st and Aug. 26th. The latter came to hand yesterday enclosing the $100—The time expired that I had borrowed the money for: having depended on Clarke's return before this. I had limited the time to 6 weeks from 3rd Aug. but his non-arrival made the rec't of yours quite opportune. The Post Master Mr. Lincoln is very careless about leaving his office open & unlocked during the day—half the time I go in & get my papers etc. without anyone being there as was the case yesterday. The letter was only marked 25 & even if he had been there & known it was double, he would not [have] charged me any more*—luckily he is a very clever fellow and a particular friend of mine. If he is there when I carry this to the office I will get him to "frank" it—

With completion of his lengthy and informative letter, Marsh again went to the New Salem post office. This time the postmaster was there, and he responded to Marsh's request by franking the bulky and expensive letter. In ink in the upper right corner he wrote: "Free. A. Lincoln P.M. New Salem Ill. Sept 22." Before leaving the store that day Marsh probably also said a word about another job the postmaster was scheduled to do for him, surveying a ten-acre piece of timberland Marsh had just bought. Two days later Lincoln took his horse and his instruments and completed the task, noting on the plat, "Timber land surveyed by A. Lincoln from Wm Green to M.S. Marsh, 24 Sept. 1835."

Eventually Marsh married (the bride was a local girl named Martha Short), moved his residence several times, worked briefly as a school-teacher, then became a successful merchant. At last he settled in booming Chicago where, having raised a large family, he died about 1890. All this time his letter of 1835 stayed in his family's possession, effectively locked away from Lincoln scholars, and for another forty years after his death. It was then turned up by the relentless William Barton, close on the heels of his triumph with Sally Saunders in California. In an address delivered at the restored New Salem in 1926, Barton made prompt use of his find, reading it whole to an audience of professional historians, along with some personal interpretation.

The offhand reference in the letter to Lincoln, he explained, quite handily disposed of the notion of Lincoln's excessive grieving at Ann's death. Young Marsh was writing only three weeks after that sad event,

---

*Postage at the time was paid by the recipient.

Signatures of some of Lincoln's New Salem friends, perhaps a voter list of the early 1830s. At left are James Rutledge (Ann's father), John (Jack) Armstrong, and Bowling Green. At right are John McNeil (Ann's other suitor), Samuel Hill, and William Green. *(Illinois State Historical Library)*

Uncle Jimmy Short,
Lincoln's good friend, was a
neighbor of the Rutledge
family at Sandridge where
Ann died.

Nancy, wife of New Salem's
Bowling Green, who recalled
caring for the grief-stricken
Lincoln for weeks in her
home.

Mentor Graham, New Salem schoolmaster, was one of the first to speak to Herndon, reporting what Abe and Ann had told him.

William Green in later life. He clerked in the Lincoln general store at New Salem and later became a wealthy and influential Illinois landowner with interests in banking and railroading.

Isaac Cogdal of New Salem and Springfield. A Lincoln law protégé, he claimed to have had a crucial conversation with president-elect Lincoln on the subject of his love for Ann Rutledge.

Samuel Hill, another unsuccessful suitor for the hand of Ann Rutledge. He married Parthena Nance, perhaps Ann's closest friend.

Parthena Nance Hill. She remembered a certain letter received by Ann.

The Hill's cabin at New Salem (modern restoration) was the only two-story structure in the village. *(Historic Sites Division, Illinois Historic Preservation Agency)*

Mary Owens, a young woman of intelligence and breeding, a year after Ann's death refused an offer of marriage from Lincoln. She is shown here at about age thirty-five.

Ann Rutledge of Ottumwa, Iowa, a great-grandniece of Lincoln's
Ann, in a 1938 photograph. On the New York stage that year, in a
play about Lincoln, she filled the role of her famous ancestor.

Inside front cover and title page (right) of the original *Kirkham's Grammar* used by both Abe and Ann. See the appendix for a discussion. *(Library of Congress)*

ENGLISH GRAMMAR,

IN

FAMILIAR LECTURES,

ACCOMPANIED BY

A COMPENDIUM:

EMBRACING

A NEW SYSTEMATICK ORDER OF PARSING,

A NEW SYSTEM OF PUNCTUATION, EXERCISES IN FALSE SYNTAX,

AND

A KEY TO THE EXERCISES:

DESIGNED

FOR THE USE OF SCHOOLS AND PRIVATE LEARNERS.

BY SAMUEL KIRKHAM.

SIXTH EDITION,

ENLARGED AND MUCH IMPROVED.

CINCINNATI:

PUBLISHED BY N. & G. GUILFORD, AT THEIR BOOK
FRANKLIN'S HEAD, 14, LOWER MARKET STREET.

W. M. & O. FARNSWORTH, JR. PRINTERS.

1828.

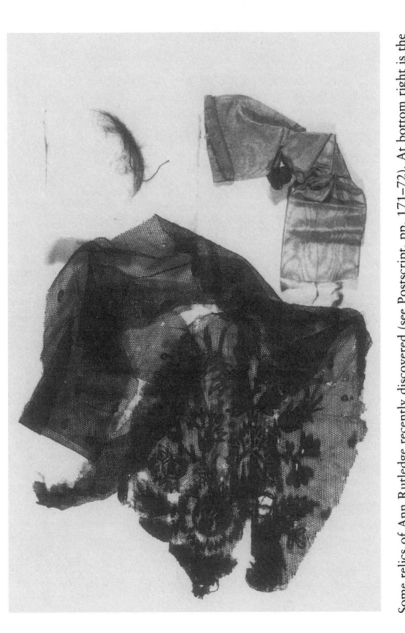

Some relics of Ann Rutledge recently discovered (see Postscript, pp. 171–72). At bottom right is the yellow silk bow, curved around the acorn button. Above the bow is the small lock of hair. The black lace, nearly two feet long, is somewhat damaged.

yet he "had no question in his mind of Lincoln's ability to attend to his duties as postmaster." In fact, Barton insisted, Marsh actually furnished proof that Lincoln "did so attend to them, franking his letter in a firm hand." The survey done for Marsh a week later also showed Lincoln to be "apparently normal so far as measurements, computation, draughtsmanship and penmanship can disclose the condition of a mind." Thus Barton became the first to invoke Marsh's casual paragraph against the legend—and also the first, though not the last, to miss completely what must be seen as the Marsh letter's true import. (The mishandling of the Marsh letter in the Rutledge context, to speak frankly, amounts to a classic case of scholarly self-delusion, if not something yet more serious.)

Far from proving Lincoln's emotional stability at the time, far from showing him engaged in his normal, everyday activities, when measured against his known character and temperament, the Marsh observations prove just the opposite. Beyond any doubt, they supply an unwitting portrait in little of a disturbed personality.

Judging by what is known of his life at New Salem, a truly normal Lincoln would not have been so carelessly absent from his proper station, leaving the U.S. mails open and unguarded. A normal Lincoln would not have impressed anyone as being ready and willing to cheat the government on the matter of postage due. A normal Lincoln would not have so readily misused his personal franking privileges, actually a matter of criminal illegality. All these things—each separately but more so when viewed collectively—unerringly reveal the operation of those subtle distortions of character often incident to spells of clinical melancholia. Of special relevance in this connection is the nickname "Honest Abe," for its bestowal actually dates to Lincoln's New Salem days. It was precisely in recognition of his exact, rigid, and unfailing honesty, present even in the smallest transactions, that the name was given him by the somewhat astonished villagers. The grocery clerk who closed his shop and walked six miles to return an overcharge of a few pennies, or who took another long walk to deliver four ounces of tea mistakenly withheld from a buyer, is not the man described by Matthew Marsh.

A curious parallel to the scholarly fumbling over the Marsh letter is the equally surprising neglect of another revealing aspect of Lincoln's career at New Salem: the marked change in personality that settled over him at, or soon after, Ann's death (more precisely, the change that became noticeable about the time he left New Salem for good). Here is a fact that stands as well attested as any deriving from Lincoln's youth, one obviously of large importance, yet it is seldom admitted more than in passing. That the Lincoln who moved to Springfield in the spring of 1837 was a changed man, decidedly more sober in manner and intellect than the young man who had been the social favorite of every New Salem group, was something evident to many of his friends at the time. Two of these in particular, Stephen Logan and Charles Matheny, both of Springfield, along with several others who were in a position to notice, may be cited here. Of course, it will always remain a question as to just how much of the alteration flowed from the normal processes of maturation—for instance, his new associations in the legislature at Vandalia—and how much to the blow he sustained at Ann's death.

Perhaps no one better than Row Herndon has described in brief Lincoln's youthful personality, giving a portrait that is readily seconded by many of those in the village. The talkative and always accessible Lincoln, said Herndon, "was of a Drole singular pleasant manner... fond of company & all that knew him sout his company, for he was all Life and humor & full of anecdotes." Here is the early Lincoln, unfailingly bright and cheerful and ready to amuse, almost ebullient. Obviously missing from the portrait is the element of reserve, the tendency to moments of brooding, the inward-looking air now so familiar. That the transition—what may legitimately be styled the deepening—took place at this time was a fact quickly noted by one of the men who knew him best, his second law partner, Stephen Logan. Acquainted with Lincoln since the summer of 1832, when both did service against Black Hawk, Logan frankly pictured him while at New Salem as a "sort of loafer."[*] The subsequent change he observed in the raw youth he describes as fundamental: "While he was down there at New Salem I think his time was mainly given to fun & social enjoyment & in the amusements he daily came in contact with. After he came here to Springfield, however, he got rid to a great degree of this disposition."

The second Springfield friend, Charles Matheny, a man who was long involved in city government, later recalled that while Lincoln had been the center of attention in the little village, that situation had

---

[*]Hannah Armstrong, Jack's wife, used the same term. "He was always a good loafer," her son heard her say more than once.

changed: "The people of New Salem would flock to hear him—loving jokes, humor, etc. This quality of his nature declined. When he first came among us [meaning his visits to Springfield from New Salem before he moved there] his wit and humor boiled over."

Others who were aware of the change were more inclined to credit ordinary human and natural pressures with bringing it about, particularly politics. One of these was A. Y. Ellis of Petersburg, who not only records the change but in the process fixes its approximate date. Writing to Herndon in 1865, Ellis comments, "I always thought that Mr. Lincoln improved rapidly in mind and manners after his return from Vandalia & his first session in the legislature." It was in mid-February 1835 that Lincoln finished his first three-month session at Vandalia, and Ellis's memory might well have been off the mark by six months or so, putting the "rapid" alteration just at or just after the time of Ann's death.

Further contemporary testimony comes from one of Ann's own friends, the woman who may have been tutoring her that last summer of her life for entrance into the Female Academy at Jacksonville. This was Arminda Rogers of Athens, whose large and well-educated family was known to and quite friendly with the Rutledges. To her own inquisitive son in succeeding years, Arminda, then Mrs. Rankin, many times told the sad story of Abe and Ann, recalled from her personal knowledge, and in December of 1866 Henry Rankin relayed to Herndon what he remembered of his mother's words. The style of the young Rankin's prose is inflated, but behind the overblown language can be heard the calmer note of Arminda's memories (she was alive at the time though quite elderly). After the young Lincoln met and fell in love with Ann, wrote Rankin, tragedy struck,

> blackening with temporary despair the once love-lit future, sobering him with sickening, rebellious thoughts, and flinging his soul back on itself, there finding himself and his God, and so changing the rollicking life to the calm, deep-reasoning soul that made a philosopher of a jovial, hail-fellow-well-met citizen of Salem. . . . This is the great transition my mother tells me she saw in the mind and character of Mr Lincoln. . . . he met his first love in the sweet and winsome personality of Ann Rutledge. Then came an incident—shall I call it only such?—Death! that flings his nature away from its old moorings, and he was lost for a brief period until he

entered a new life—rare in this world of ours—of silence, as you and I have often seen him.

Another quite telling bit of evidence on the subduing of the Lincoln personality, this one preserved wholly by accident, relates to the period just subsequent to Ann's passing, apparently a matter of days after the encounter with Matthew Marsh. The obscure anecdote was recorded in 1879 by Usher Linder, a longtime political friend of Lincoln. Its link to the Rutledge legend previously unrecognized, it shows Lincoln in the act of paying one of his rare visits to his parents in their home near Charleston in Coles County, Illinois. The date of the visit as indicated by Linder is the fall of 1835, almost certainly October. In no way highlighted in the simple narrative, the passage occurs in Linder's *Reminiscences,* a work that shows a very careful attention to details of chronology (Linder dates the incident by reference to two events in his own life: his ill health at the time and the death of a little son in a fever epidemic, perhaps the same one that took Ann). Prevented by his illness, as he says, from traveling the law circuit in fall 1835, he attended court at Charleston instead. There he first met Lincoln, who struck him at the time as being "a very modest and retiring man," nothing like the voluble and unfailing source of fun and pleasantry known to New Salemites:

> he did not make any marked impression upon me, or any other member of the bar. He was on a visit to his relatives in Coles, where his father and stepmother lived, and some of her children. Lincoln put up at the hotel, and there was where I saw him. Whether he was reading law at this time I cannot say. Certain it is, he had not then been admitted to the bar,[*] although he had some celebrity, having been a captain in the Black-Hawk campaign, and served a term in the legislature. . . .
>
> I had known his relatives in Kentucky, and he asked me about them. His uncle, Mordecai Lincoln, I had known from my boyhood, and he was naturally a man of considerable genius; he was a man of great drollery, and it would almost make you laugh to look at him. . . . The impression that Mr. Lincoln made upon me when I first saw him at the hotel in Charleston, was very slight. He had the appearance of a good-natured, easy, unambitious man, of

---

[*]Lincoln's certification as a lawyer took place officially in March 1836.

plain good sense, and unobtrusive in his manners. At that time he told me no stories and perpetrated no jokes.

The two men are relaxing in the amiable atmosphere of a small-town hotel. They are talking, no doubt among other things, of Lincoln's wonderfully humorous uncle, a man Lincoln admired greatly and always recalled with special fondness (he once said that Mordecai had "run off with all the talents" of the family). But from Lincoln himself on that occasion came none of his own jokes and funny stories, nothing in the way of high spirits, no hint of the homey charm that had so taken his New Salem neighbors. The whole impression made on Linder by this tall, conspicuous figure of a twenty-six-year-old, with his long, thin neck, rugged face prematurely lined, and thick, unruly black hair, a young man who usually struck those he met as quite out of the ordinary, was "very slight." But that is a surprising outcome of the meeting only until it is recalled what had happened in the young man's life some weeks before: the girl he loved had died, and here he was, downcast and unaccountably sober, coming for a visit to the poor, lonely log-cabin home of his parents. That he was looking for solace in his heartbreak at his old home is a legitimate inference even under the most rigid historical constraints. Particularly from his stepmother would he have sought and expected sympathy, for her sensibilities, as she herself admitted, always "seemed to run together" with his.

William Herndon has been faulted for many things, most of them undeserved. But here is a truly grievous omission. In the fall of 1865, in the course of his researches he called on Lincoln's stepmother, then widowed but still living in a Coles County cabin. Incredibly, not a single question did he ask the venerable old lady about Ann Rutledge, never even asked whether she had heard the name.

ら

No document remains, contemporary with New Salem days, linking directly and unequivocally the names of Abraham Lincoln and Ann Rutledge. Closest, at least in possibility, is an old grammar textbook supposedly used by both. Though it perhaps adds little to the picture of their romantic involvement, it is worth a brief look, connected as it is with their wish to prepare for a future together by repairing their defective educations.

The day after Lincoln's temporary burial at Springfield, on May 4,

1865, the *Illinois State Journal* on page 2 carried the following squib:

> *An Interesting Relic.*—We were yesterday shown by some gentlemen from Iowa the identical "Kirkham's Grammar" which Mr. Lincoln studied while living in Petersburg, Menard County, Illinois, about the year 1830. It was presented by Mr. Lincoln to the present Capt. R. B. Rutledge, now of Burlington, Iowa, with whose father Mr. Lincoln boarded at the time. We are told it originally bore upon a fly-leaf the name of Abraham Lincoln, with these not unfamiliar lines, "Steal not this book, etc." but this has been torn out by subsequent usage. The volume, which is highly valued for its associations, is still the property of Capt. Rutledge.

Several days later the same paper printed a letter it received from Captain Rutledge himself, one of those "gentlemen from Iowa" who had brought the book to Springfield. After correcting the error about Lincoln living at Petersburg, Robert explained that the volume had been given by Lincoln not to him but "to an elder sister, Ann M. Rutledge." That very book, he added, "has been studied by myself and other members of our family." Among the several interesting aspects of this first public linking of the names of Abe and Ann is this: it occurred a year and a half *prior* to Herndon's Rutledge lecture, and almost the same length of time before Herndon was in touch with the Rutledge family.

As it happened, this same book had received some public notice even before the *Journal* mention, in a Lincoln campaign biography written by W. D. Howells, published in the summer of 1860. Drawing on information supplied by several New Salem residents, Howells wrote that while at New Salem Lincoln had begun his self-education, and "the first branch of learning which he took up was English Grammar, acquiring that science from the dry and meager treatise of Kirkham. The book was not to be had in the immediate vicinity, and Lincoln walked seven or eight miles to acquire a copy."

Lincoln's long walk to borrow the book was confirmed to Herndon in 1865, some three weeks after the *Journal* story, when he had his second interview with Mentor Graham in Petersburg. Lincoln, Graham explained, had one day mentioned that he had

a notion of studying grammar. I replied to him thus, "If you ever expect to go before the public in any capacity I think it the best thing you can do." He said to me "If I had a grammar I would commence now." There was none in the village & I said to him, "I know of a grammar at one Vance's about 6 miles" which I thought he could get. He was then at breakfast—ate—got up and went on foot to Vance's and got the Book. He soon came back and told me he had it. He then turned his inordinate and almost undivided attention to English grammar. The book was Kirkham's Grammar—an old volume that I suppose—have so heard—is in the Rutledge family today.

The Vance mentioned by Graham was a real resident of New Salem, John C. Vance, who lived some way north of the village. That Lincoln knew him is established by mention of the man in a Lincoln letter written at the time of Vance's death early in 1835.

The actual Kirkham's volume in question was preserved in the Rutledge family for decades, being used for study in turn by David, Jane, Nancy, Robert, and Sarah. "I studied that very grammar afterward when I went to school," Nancy recalled. "Lincoln and Ann studied it together, and he gave it to her, and it then descended to my brother, and then to me.... many a time have I seen Lincoln walking along the street of New Salem studying that grammar."

After its brief round of publicity following Lincoln's death, the volume dropped out of sight, to turn up again in 1895 in possession of Robert's widow, when its title page was photographed for use by Tarbell. In 1922 it was donated on extended loan by William Rutledge, Robert's son, to the public library of Decatur, Illinois. Ten years after that it found a permanent resting place at the Library of Congress.[*]

Fittingly, the ancient but well-preserved volume—it was published in 1828 at Cincinnati—does present at least one small mystery. Written in ink along the top edge of the title page is the name "Ann M. Rutledge." This is followed on two separate lines by the phrase, also in ink, "is now learning Grammar." For a long time it was believed that the handwriting was Lincoln's, though in truth its neatly rounded script little resembles his clear if spidery hand. Quite definitely the writing is not Lincoln's. Whose then? There are those who like to think that these graceful letters were formed by Ann's own hand, making the

---

[*]See the appendix for further on the original *Kirkham's* volume.

Kirkham's text the only personal relic of the young woman to have survived. Perhaps on receiving the book from Lincoln's hands she wrote the impulsive sentence out of a mixture of surprise and delight at the happy future that seemed to beckon.

ৈ

Why did John McNamar leave so little on record about himself and Ann when he might have told so much? What perverse fate was it that kept him away from his New Salem home and his promised bride for the length of three full years? Complete answers to such nagging questions are perhaps no longer to be expected. Yet it is possible even now, after all that has been written, to make some small addition to the store of information on each. The effort is surely worthwhile, for if McNamar had returned to New Salem in good time, say even as late as the fall of 1833, he and Ann might have married as planned and there would have been no Rutledge legend to roil the inspiring tale of Lincoln's beginnings.

It was the illness and death of his father, McNamar said, that had been the major cause of his continued absence. This in turn had created a further delay in the need to look after his bereft family, a fact he slightly expanded on in the last of his letters to Herndon. Much more of hardship and tragedy was involved, it appears, than the loss of an elderly father: "One of those long interminable fevers that some-times occur in the east came into my Father's family & prostrated every member, that is except myself, and continued for months, mak-ing victims of three of them, one of whom was my Father." As it happens, still in existence is the account book of Dr. Timothy Bancroft, a physician of Colesville, New York, active in the 1830s. On two of its handwritten and slightly confused pages is preserved the record of Dr. Bancroft's attendance on the McNamara family for nearly three months at the start of 1833, between January and April.* The tale told by the simple listing of calls and fees fully supports McNamar's thirty-year memory.

Three sons, David, George, and Andrew, are named as patients along with the father. During the period covered by the two pages no

---

*The family always retained the final *a* on the name, for some reason dropped by John. The spelling in any case was rather loose, for the father's tombstone is inscribed *McNamarah*.

less than eighty-one house calls are entered. Several times two or even three visits occur on a single day, and there are occasional mentions of a consultant being called in, one Dr. Bronson. On March 31 George died, to be followed some weeks later by one of the other two boys. That the family's awful burden did not cease with the depressing story told by the account book is clear from the fact that the date of death on the father's tombstone in Coles Hill Cemetery reads "April 10, 1833," which is two days after the final entry in the ledger. Each of Dr. Bancroft's visits to the house cost between fifty cents and a dollar and a quarter, not counting medicines, and on July 15 the bill was settled up to April 8 for $63.50. A separate notation by the doctor, made some unknown length of time later, reads, "Moved to Petersburg, Illinois."

Granted that this terrible visitation on the McNamara family, would have left even the survivors prostrate for a good while, certainly in spirit, the question still arises: if John McNamar eventually took his reduced family back with him to New Salem, why could he not have done so sooner? What explains the passing of two long years after abatement of the fever scourge in his household before he made his move west?

Starting with what is known, it may be accepted that McNamar's clear purpose in visiting New York State was simply to rescue his debt-ridden family and then return with them—father, mother, and several brothers and sisters—to Illinois where he had prepared a farm to receive them. Traveling by horseback, he left New Salem in August or early September 1832, at the latest, and arrived at his parents' home in New York perhaps toward the end of October. To prepare so many people for the long journey back, some considerable time would have been needed, and the party could scarcely have meant to travel in winter. McNamar's original hope, then, may have been for a safe arrival back at Sandridge by May or June 1833.

So much seems likely, and in that case Ann could have looked forward to the return of her fiancé and to meeting her prospective in-laws after a wait of only some eight or nine months, not unreasonable. But with the descent of wholesale illness on the family in New York that spring and summer—beginning, say, five or six weeks after McNamar's arrival—these plans were abandoned. Before there could have been any renewed thought of departing for the Midwest, it would have been late in 1833 and again verging on winter. The documented family illness thus readily accounts for a delay until the spring of 1834, and it is here that the original question may be pressed: what was it that caused a final postponement to the summer of 1835?

In answer to that question there are two obvious possibilities, either of which will serve. The widowed and perhaps dispirited Mrs. McNamara, rebelling at the thought of consigning her remaining children to the uncertainties of a frontier life (the Black Hawk War was then still very fresh in memory), may simply have refused to go. In that case, her eldest son, now the family's head, would scarcely have abandoned her. Also possible is a change in McNamar himself. After two years' sojourn back in the civilized East, he may have had second thoughts about locating permanently so far from settled surroundings. If so, his doubts on this score may in turn have led him to change his mind about the girl he had left waiting in a rough log cabin on the prairie. When compared with the accomplished young women of his familiar New York village, the rustic Ann, in McNamar's recollection, could well have lost some of her attraction (in his later note to Herndon he shows himself as quite aware that Ann had been "without any of the airs of your City Belles"). If either of these conditions were in operation for a period of time—perhaps both of them together, one enforcing the other—they sufficiently account for the fact that it was July 1835 before minds were again altered, and McNamar and his family packed all their goods into a wagon and headed west.

At this juncture, satisfyingly, speculation may be put aside, for there exist two documents relating to McNamar's arrival back in New Salem that help greatly to clarify the always hitherto confused and incomplete ending to the story. Both documents derive from the by then aged Parthena Hill, widow of New Salem merchant Samuel Hill and perhaps Ann's closest friend. The first is a revealing interview she gave Herndon in 1887 (still strangely little referred to), the second a letter of 1896 to her son John which apparently has remained entirely overlooked. Brief statements in the two documents show that just before Ann fell victim to the fever epidemic then raging in the area she received a letter from McNamar announcing his imminent return. Convincingly, Mrs. Hill dates the occurrence by reference to her own marriage in July 1835.

Herndon's notes of the 1887 interview, held twenty years after his lecture and while he was preparing his Lincoln biography, have Mrs. Hill saying that Ann, after hearing nothing for a year, "got a letter from McNamar telling her to be ready etc. to be married." Nothing further on the point was said at that interview, but the later letter confirms all that the woman said earlier. It also adds a telling detail, one that would have been well calculated to disturb and upset the ailing Ann. The absent fiancée, notes Mrs. Hill to her son,

> had <u>overstaid</u> his <u>appointed</u> time. Ann got a letter from him just before she took sick, saying <u>be ready</u>—he would buy furniture in Cincinnati and wanted to be married as soon as he got here, and go to housekeeping.

Undoubtedly, Ann's hope had been to announce to the returned McNamar, in the calmest and quickest manner, the alteration in her feelings for him, as well as her intention to marry another man. But now came the news that the unsuspecting lover would be arriving very shortly and with a pile of furniture in tow, eagerly anticipating an immediate wedding—at that juncture there would have been no chance, of course, to reach him before he left New York.

To the gentle Ann, the thought of the severe disappointment she would be causing her old love, not to mention the resulting public embarrassment he would suffer, must have been vastly troubling. As she awaited McNamar's arrival her brooding on what promised to be an extremely distasteful denouement, souring for the moment her plans with Lincoln, could not have missed further unsettling her fevered mind. Here, certainly, is the origin and true basis of Herndon's naive idea that Ann died out of mortification over the clash of her two engagements. That she actually died during a fever epidemic in the area might, with a little effort, have been discovered by Herndon, supporting the claim of Robert Rutledge that the cause was "brain fever." In any case, full confirmation of that fact has for years been handily available. Charles Clarke of New Salem, friend of Matthew Marsh, on October 4, 1835, wrote a letter home in which he remarks that "it has ben very sickly this season through all the western country two or three deaths in our neighborhood and a great many cases of sickness generally chills and fevers and bilious fevers." If Clarke thought of Sandridge as being in his "neighborhood," which is likely, then Ann's death must be counted among the "two or three" fatalities he mentions.*

---

*Marsh himself, in his long letter to his parents of September 17 that same year—the letter franked by Lincoln—remarked that "there has been more sickness this summer than ever was known before."

Another small detail in Mrs. Hill's letter is particularly compelling, for it surely reflects the moment when the shocked McNamar found that the woman he expected to marry was already dead and buried. On his arrival at New Salem, McNamar "unloaded his furniture at Dr. Allen's just across the street from us, and one bedstead stood against the house for days before it was taken in." The forgotten bedstead propped against Dr. Allen's rear wall (in the restored village it is plainly visible from the windows of the Hill place) may stand as a forlorn emblem of the fate that had overtaken and drastically altered the lives of two men. Dr. John Allen, close friend and business partner of McNamar, was probably the physician who attended Ann.

Yet another very useful purpose is served by Mrs. Hill's letter to her son, for it helps to clarify the tangled question of a formal engagement between Abe and Ann. If McNamar expected to marry Ann on his return, then it is certain that the young woman had never written him of her change of heart, had told him nothing of her new suitor. This omission in turn strongly suggests that the actual engagement—its reality can scarcely be any longer doubted—had been only recently concluded. Perhaps the new arrangement was not made definite until some time in the late spring of 1835, not long before Ann fell sick. Because of the timing, and the swift piling up of events, it may not have been publicly announced before Ann entered the crisis. That would account for the slight disagreement on the topic among several of Herndon's informants and for those such as James Short who claimed they had heard nothing official about an engagement. It also makes it easier to believe McNamar's somewhat puzzling disclaimer: he had, he said, "never heard any person say that Mr. Lincoln addressed Miss Ann Rutledge in terms of courtship neither her own family nor my acquaintances otherwise." While Ann's acceptance of Lincoln certainly was known informally to most of those close to the couple, since it had never been made official no one wished, just then, to add to McNamar's burden of shock by telling him that the dead Ann had ceased to care for him. His own unaltered feelings are sufficiently evident in two of his first actions on reaching home. He set a wooden cross at the head of Ann's unmarked, still fresh grave, and when he was shown a lock of her hair he asked to have a portion.

That McNamar eventually discovered the truth, at least in part, may be taken as certain—especially since he lived on in the area—though it may not have been until long afterward. That he thereafter grew reluctant to talk openly of that early rejection is understandable, if unfortunate in the long view of history. His last recorded words on the girl, more than ever laconic, were delivered in his old age. "She was fair and her form well rounded," he told a reporter who visited his Sandridge farm in 1874. "She had blue eyes and auburn hair. She was kind and cheerful. When I came back from a long business trip to the east she was buried. You passed her grave by the little white church yonder."

ᶻ▲

The tradition of Lincoln's farewell call at Ann's deathbed has been a part of the legend from the start, deriving mostly from her brother Robert. But two of her sisters, Nancy and Sarah, in reply to direct inquiries also left statements on record concerning that final visit. Not much in the way of significant detail is added, yet their brief recollections do manage to make more vivid—mostly by what they do *not* say—a tableau that must stand as one of the more affecting and portentous in American history.

"I can never forget," recalled Nancy, picturing an event she had witnessed at age fifteen, "how sad and broken-hearted Lincoln looked when he came out of the room from the last interview with Annie. No one knows what was said at that meeting, for they were alone together." As with all the other members of her family, Nancy stoutly resisted what must have been a very strong temptation to embroider. In her statement she included something she heard later, and apparently believed, but referred it to another source. Lincoln, she said, "told a friend that she told him always to live an honest and upright life." If only Nancy had named the friend.

Sarah's memories of the same event, expressed in several letters, were written in her old age, a fact to which she herself meticulously calls attention. Even as she describes it, she admits that the memory is "dimly seen," and she is unsure whether she is recalling talk later heard around the house or an event actually witnessed by her own childish eyes:

> I am sorry to have so little recollection of the time you speak about, being a mere child of six or seven. Of course there are some events that took place that will remain with me as long as my memory lasts. I can recall the times I saw Lincoln at our table

and fireside. But any incident or act connected with him I do not clearly retain. I remember when we left New Salem for my father's farm and while there both Father and sister Ann fell sick, [and] that my Mother could be seen waiting on them both. I heard them say how sick they were and that sister Ann grew worse as the days passed by. Finally my brother David who was attending school in Jacksonville, Ill., and Lincoln were sent for. I can see them as they each came, and when Lincoln went into the sick room where sister Ann lay, the others retired. A few minutes later Lincoln came from the room with bowed head and seemed to me at the time to be crying. Soon after this Ann died.

As Nancy and Sarah both specify, Lincoln's farewell call at the bedside of the dying Ann was made alone, only the two of them in the room. This in itself strongly argues a special relationship, one duly recognized and accommodated by the anguished family. Sarah's saying that her sister died "soon after" that final call need not mean that Lincoln went away before Ann breathed her last. More likely he remained at the Rutledges or in the vicinity until the end, also attending the funeral at the old Concord Cemetery. Given the gentle Ann's popularity among all sorts, the funeral party round the gravesite would have been a large one, with Lincoln's tall, thin figure rising above the rest.

None of the Rutledges corroborated any of the details of Lincoln's "crazy spell," or his supposed suicidal tendencies. Nancy, in fact, commenting on this aspect of the story, insisted she had "never heard any of our family" talk of such abandoned behavior on Lincoln's part, and she added the familiar lament that "there are so many things in the papers which are not true." Yet she did accept, certainly by reason of her own knowledge on the point, the repeated assertions that had Lincoln confessing to his friends, "My heart lies buried with that girl," or similar words. A fifteen-year-old, hearing such an anguished cry burst from the lips of a sorrowing lover, especially concerning her own sister, might well carry the memory of it for a lifetime. But there is nothing in those words, so sadly despairing, that need offend the guardians of Lincoln's reputation. Under the stress of overwhelming loss anyone might feel and speak this way, and at the moment of utterance the thought is quite sincerely believed. Seldom does it accurately predict the future, however, nor as a calm review of the evidence in these pages shows—along with the events of his whole subsequent life and career—did it do so in Lincoln's case.

Yet neither was it entirely false.

Abraham Lincoln did undoubtedly love Ann Rutledge. She, in turn, as was testified by her mother, by her brothers and sisters, and by many others who knew both, loved him. He would certainly have married her, and that thought calls up intense curiosity as to what direction in that case his life might have taken, curiosity never to be satisfied.

When Ann died in all her youth and loveliness, surely some portion of Lincoln's sorely grieving heart, as he said, descended with her fever-wasted body into the grave. Just as surely, the tragedy and shock of her passing left him for some days or weeks mentally distraught, then for months in a state of emotional abeyance, finally taking away much of his earlier joyous feeling for life. His often-noted, lifelong melancholic strain—even if the tendency was inborn—thus in some part may be said to have had a specific origin in wrenching personal grief. Further, those who choose to see this youthful turmoil of spirit as in some mysterious way contributing to Lincoln's greatness—humanly and as a statesman—should not be lightly contradicted.

Here is no radical or startling admission, no cause for controversy. It only repeats what everyone with any experience of life knows all too well, that such tragedies do happen, no doubt more often than is guessed. Invariably they leave their mark, serious or shallow, according to circumstances and to the personal temperament of the unfortunate sufferer.

From all that is known, Lincoln appears to have been little different from the many others whom fate has chosen for the experience. Sobered in outlook and with passion subdued, they almost always recover and go on to love again, readily managing to live normal, happy, even highly successful lives. Nor is it at all surprising that the memory of such a lost love might continue unfading through a lifetime, in a silent corner of the heart to be ever more idealized as the years drop away.

Appendix: The Original
Kirkham's Grammar

As it exists today in the Rare Book Division of the Library of Congress, the copy of *Kirkham's Grammar* used by Lincoln, and later by Ann, is in good condition generally. Its light-brown leather cover well preserved, it shows only the usual signs of wear. But it holds several features of interest not before put on record.*

Affixed to the inside front cover, as is well known, is a receipt written and signed by Lincoln on behalf of his New Salem employer Denton Offutt ("Mr. James Rutledge please to pay the bearer David P. Nelson thirty dollars and this shall be your receipt for the same. March 8th 1832"). Pasted down by a strip along its outer edge, the receipt lifts up to reveal the inside front cover itself. Here, written prominently in ink, is the name "Miller Arrowsmith," accompanied by the notation "Commenced studying of Kirkham's Grammar June 8th 1829."† Nowhere in the extant New Salem documents or in books and articles on the topic does the name of Arrowsmith come up. But apparently this unknown young man (the handwriting is youthful) was the book's first owner. If Lincoln did procure his copy from John

---

*This discussion is based on an examination of the volume by John C. Walsh, Humanities Librarian, Fenwick Library, George Mason University, to whom I am grateful.

†In light of this entry, and those that follow, I am at a loss to explain an earlier report by Ida Tarbell. In 1922, while the book was still at the Decatur, Ill., library, she made an examination of it, as she says, "page by page." Her findings: "Never was a book, although studied by many different people, more respectfully treated. There is not a written word in Lincoln's or anybody else's hand, aside from those on the title page and cover" (*Footsteps,* 177).

Vance, as Mentor Graham claimed, then it was secondhand when Vance received it.

Also written on the inside front cover are two other names, both with connections to Lincoln. First is that of Ann's sister Sarah (Sally). It appears twice—"Sarah F. Rutledge"—both times in pencil, in a hand obviously that of a child. Sarah was born in 1829, so she would have signed the book by, say, 1840, if not sooner. The date is important in confirming that the volume was owned by the Rutledge family quite early. Sarah's name appears a third time at the top of page 6.

Rather puzzling is the final name entered on the inside front cover. In ink, running down the center of the page and crossing atop the Arrowsmith entry, is the name "Daniel G. Burner" (two practice capital D's precede the first name). This was the son of Isaac Burner, one of the original New Salem settlers, with whose family Lincoln lodged for a time. Dan Burner, five years Lincoln's junior, occasionally lent a hand in the Lincoln store, and in an 1895 interview he recalled that Lincoln "was a hard student. It seemed to me he was studying all the time. . . . In the dry goods store he studied grammar." Burner's name being in the volume may indicate that he was one of those who assisted Lincoln with his studies (for instance, see L. M. Green, below, whose name also appears in the book). However, it should be noted that Burner also stated, "Lincoln and I had about the same amount of schooling and that wasn't much" (both quotations from Temple, *Herald,* 67). The latest possible date for the entry is spring 1834, the period when the Burner family departed the village to move west. (For further on Burner, see p. 162.)

Also entered on the inside front cover, unlinked to other writing, is the bare notation "August 1833." By then the book must have been in Lincoln's possession, but the writing is not his. So far as is known, nothing of special import happened to Lincoln at that date aside from his becoming involved in two minor lawsuits as a party to some promissory notes (Miers, 34–35). On the other hand, there is the known fact—it must be mentioned but without undue stress—that Ann's departure from New Salem to join her family at Sandridge did take place at about this time (see pp. 28, 69).

Since the book was not returned to Vance, it is unlikely that Lincoln *borrowed* it, though he may later have worked off its cost, or Vance could have given it to him. It is also possible that Lincoln did borrow a copy from Vance, then returned it and purchased a copy of his own, the present volume. In the *Sangamon Journal* for most of 1833 the book was advertised for sale at a Springfield bookstore. Perhaps Lincoln bought a secondhand copy, which would explain the Arrowsmith inscription, of which there is a second entry, on the inside *back* cover: "Miller Arrowsmith / is my name / on my conduct I'll / build my fame."

Several other handwritten inscriptions occur throughout the book.* Page 5 in pencil has this: "Martha B. Berry is now learning Gramer." Evidently this refers to a daughter of Ann's older sister Jane. Married in 1829, Jane Berry had nine children, but none of their birthdates is readily available.

Worthy of special note is an entry, in ink, along the top of page 153: "L. M. Green." This is Lynn McNulty Green (see p. 99), who on two different occasions stated that he had helped Lincoln with his studies. In an interview of 1860 he said, "Every time I went to Salem he took me out on the hill & got me to explain to him *Kirkham*" (Mearns, 156). Writing to Herndon in 1865 Green explained how Lincoln "got possession of one of *Kirkham's* grammars & began studying on the hillsides of Old Salem. I spent several days giving him instruction" (July 30, 1865, reel 9). Lynn or Nult Green had no particular link to the Rutledge family, so he would have had practically no access to the book afterward, certainly not to insert his name. Thus it appears that the Green signature may well have been written in while Lincoln himself was present, during one of their hillside study sessions.

Of the inscription on the title page, "Ann M. Rutledge is now learning Grammar," there is little definite to be said except that it is by a practiced hand. Whoever wrote it was aware that Ann's middle name was Mayes, though that information could have come from Ann herself at the time of writing. If it is not Ann's own hand, then some obvious possibilities are her parents as well as her two teachers, Mentor Graham (it does not much resemble his ordinary hand of later years) and Arminda Rogers (no sample of her hand is available). Her elder sister, Jean, and her elder brother, John, are remoter possibilities. In any case, the presence of Ann's name so prominently on the title page shows that she owned the book and had not just borrowed it. The way the inscription is written seems to show that the words following the name were an afterthought: the name is centered above the title, the other four words straggle between and around the lines of type (see the illustration). Who might have presumed to add those four words? The "now" is perhaps a clue, indicating that Ann was just then *beginning* her studies, which may point to Arminda Rogers (see pp. 102, 167).

The provenance of the volume is not easily worked out. Ann would have had it for perhaps a year, during which time others in the Rutledge home no doubt made use of it. From Ann it seems to have gone to her brother David, and on his death in 1842 it went to Jean, for use by her large brood. Next it went to Nancy, mother of four, and from her in 1865 to Robert, who exhibited it at the Lincoln funeral in Springfield. Nancy, in

---

*I make no effort to detail all such entries, for instance, the phrase "english grammar" on page 33 and what appears to be the name "Friday" on page 43.

1886, said that she had kept it until her brother "went to Springfield to assist at Lincoln's burial. He wrote me for it, as they were collecting Lincoln relics for the occassion. My brother's family has it now" (Flindt, *Inter-Ocean*).

After that, Sarah, in California, had it for a time, when it went to Robert's widow, living in Casselton, North Dakota.* She made it available to Tarbell for photographing (*Early*, 132) and eventually left it to her son William, living in Montana. In 1922, when William sent it on loan to the Decatur, Illinois, public library, it would have been worth a considerable sum. So far as is known, however, he eventually made it an outright gift. Jane Hammand of the Decatur library, the intermediary who arranged for the loan of the book, later explained what happened next: "After learning that people came from all parts of the country to see it, [Mr. Rutledge] finally wrote me that we could keep it for all time. I wrote him that while appreciating his magnanimity, I felt that there was but one place in America where it should be kept 'for all time,' and that was in the Congressional Library" (*Report of the Librarian of Congress, 1932*, 18–19).

Today, according to Clark Evans of the Library's Rare Book Division, the volume is considered among "the greatest treasures" of that treasure-crammed institution.

---

*Sarah may have had it twice. In 1919 she told an interviewer that "until recently I had an old grammar which he and Ann used to study earnestly together" (clipping, undated, from the St. Louis *Post-Dispatch*, preserved at the Lincoln Library, Fort Wayne.)

Notes and Sources

These notes are organized by chapters, and the sequence of the citations and comment follows that of the text. The page numbers are continuous, and a glance down the left-hand margin will quickly locate any item. For quoted matter the first few words of the quotation are repeated, enough to make identification sure. Citations are given in shortened form and may be fully identified by reference to the bibliography.

Prologue: Ghost Town

1 For the story of New Salem and its restoration, see in particular the works by Barton, Chandler, Onstot, Reep, and Thomas. The extensive sections on the New Salem of Lincoln's day in Beveridge, Nicolay and Hay, Tarbell, and Sandburg (discounting the fictional element), though somewhat dated, are still of value.

2 "the finest and most comprehensive"—*Catalogue,* vi. This book lists every one of the thousands of relics of daily life on display in the various buildings, with the provenance and donor's name of each. Many of the articles had actually been used at old New Salem and were sent back by descendants of the original settlers.

2 "never saw the minute"—Hertz, 123.

3 "I heard him spoken of"—Speed, 16.

4 "one of the agents"—Whitney, 169.

4 Lincoln and the Rutledge tavern—At times Lincoln boarded with the Rutledges while sleeping elsewhere (in the rear of his two stores, for example). At other times he ate and slept at the tavern. Dates for all this,

despite some assertions, are impossible to fix even approximately. When sleeping and eating elsewhere he still would have been a frequent drop-in at the tavern, which was the closest thing at New Salem to a community center.

5 "intrinsic importance"—J. Randall, 321.

5 "To spin out the analysis"—J. Randall, 341.

Chapter 1: Discovering Ann

9 Herndon's visit to the site of New Salem in October 1866 was fully described by himself in his Rutledge lecture a month later. He specifically mentions that he made notes while there ("When I wrote the original of this on my knee I was on the hill and bluff. . . . I sat down to write amid the ruins," etc.). For his descriptions of the site as quoted, see Herndon's lecture, 16–22.

11 Herndon's three prior lectures on Lincoln—For a description of these see Donald, 197–210. Donald's very readable if somewhat biased book, based on massive research, is the only full-scale biography of Herndon yet published. Its at times unfortunate portrait of its subject—Donald paints Herndon as rather a buffoon while somewhat slighting his many good qualities of intellect and spirit—has become fixed in the literature. That skewed personal portrait of Ann's discoverer is a good part of the reason for all the reluctance to take seriously his evidence on the Rutledge legend. No adequate corrective to Donald is yet at hand, though a start was made in 1991 by Douglas Wilson in a talk at the Lincoln Symposium in Springfield entitled "William Herndon and His Lincoln Informants," soon to be published.

12 "one of the world's"—Herndon's lecture, 5.

12 "records accessible to"—*Sangamon Journal,* Nov. 16, 1866.

12 The Rutledge lecture—The title varied, and this is its simplest form. Often the first line of "The Poem" was tacked on: "Oh, why should the spirit of mortal be proud?"

13 "Lincoln loved Ann"—Herndon's lecture, 3. For the next six quotations see the lecture, 4–8, 11, 24.

13 For Herndon's acute and graphic observations on the pioneers see the lecture, 27–39. His lengthy and compelling description of the typical pioneer-as-hero is particularly good.

15 "Abraham Lincoln loved Miss"—Herndon's lecture, 39. For the next six quotations see the lecture, 40–46.

18 "He saw new beauties"—Herndon's lecture, 46. Herndon is correct about Lincoln memorizing the poem. In later years he is reliably reported to have recited it complete on several occasions, and there exist at least

two manuscripts of the poem written out by him at the request of friends (Boyd, *Legacy*, xii–xvi). That it was Dr. Jason Duncan of New Salem who first showed him the poem was afterward confirmed by Lincoln himself when he told the fact to the painter F. B. Carpenter while in the White House (Carpenter, 58–59). The interesting question, of course, and one now past answering, is *when* Lincoln decided to make the considerable effort of learning all fifty-six lengthy lines of the poem. Indications are that it was before his service in Congress, but nothing more precise can be gleaned (for some speculation on the point, see Wilson, "Mortal," 163–66). The obvious link between Ann Rutledge and stanza 3 becomes even more intriguing when it is realized that in writing out the poem Lincoln—whether by accident or design—in both cases transposed the two last lines of the third stanza:

> The maid on whose cheek, on whose brow, in whose eye
> Shone beauty and pleasure, her triumphs are by;
> And alike from the minds of the living erased
> Are the mem'ries of those who loved her and praised.

In the two manuscripts he prepared for friends no other such alterations can be seen. What it may mean in this instance, if anything beyond a lapse of memory or of concentration, is hard to say.

20 "newspapers as such"—This notice is not included in the pamphlet reprint of the lecture. It did accompany the copyright notice printed at the end of newspaper reprints. Quoted here from a contemporary clipping at the Illinois State Historical Library, Springfield.

20 "melancholy and"—*New York Times,* Nov. 24, 1866.

Chapter 2: The Legend Grows

22 "would never have sought"—*Boston Advertiser,* Dec. 15, 1866, as reprinted in *New York Times,* Dec. 16, 1866. For further detail on Mrs. Dall and her visit to Springfield, see Donald, 221–23. Her error about the length of McNamar's absence from New Salem, and the reason for it, no doubt reflects Herndon's own uncertainty at the time. After Mrs. Dall left Springfield, the suddenly alarmed Herndon wrote her a request that she not make public the information on Lincoln and Ann until after his lecture. She replied on November 11 from Milwaukee assuring him that "not one word shall be written or spoken by me touching any disputed point till your lecture comes," which probably left Herndon wondering. She added, "My mind keeps at work on the subject" (original letter, Herndon-Weik Papers, reel 8-1027).

23 "rumor started that he"—*New York Tribune,* Feb. 8, 1867, as reprinted

in *New York Independent,* Feb. 28, 1867. Townsend's saying that McNamar "returned like a ghost ... and upbraided the lady with fickleness," while mistaken, is evidently linked to the remark in the Dall story about "the rumor of the recovered Scotchman's return." Both these statements, in turn, are linked to and partially explained by the facts laid out in my concluding chapter.

23 "reckless disregard"—Letter, March 6, 1867, Herndon-Weik Papers, reel 9-1456.

23 "On the dead woman's"—*New York Tribune,* Feb. 8, 1867, as reprinted in *New York Independent,* Feb. 28, 1867.

24 Mrs. Dall's article "Pioneering" appeared in *Atlantic Monthly,* April 1867, 403-16. A rambling expansion of the *Advertiser* piece, it is unsigned even though written in the first person.

24 "The love and death of"—Dall, "Pioneering," 410. Much of the article quotes Herndon directly on a variety of Lincoln and pioneer topics. some of it of real value.

25 "my duty ... my religion"—Hertz, 130.

25 Herndon and Lamon—For the transactions between these two on the Lincoln biography, see Hertz, 57-81. For the extended quotations in my text from Lamon, see that book, 159-71. To give an example of my shortening process, dropped from the Lamon text are such phrases as "that redoubtable pedagogue" and "fell unbidden from his lips." Herndon did not give Lamon the originals of his "Lincoln Record" but copies, which are now at the Huntington Library.

33 For the 1874 interview with McNamar, see pp. 168, and see also the bibliography under "Hickox." For Herndon's association with Jesse Weik, see Hertz, 183-269.

34 The original draft of Herndon's Ann Rutledge chapter in *Life* is preserved in the Herndon-Weik Papers, reel 11. Quotations in my text from *Life* are from the Da Capo reprint, 1983, pp. 105-15.

34 "She was a beautiful"—Herndon, *Life,* 106.

35 "they would have settled"—Herndon, *Life,* 109.

35 "In passing through Ohio"—Herndon, *Life,* 109.

35 "His detention necessitated"—Herndon, *Life,* 110. In this passage it appears that Herndon has substituted his imagination, or Weik's, for the facts. McNamar by then was dead, and Herndon actually knew nothing about the course of his correspondence with Ann. Evidently the gap in the narrative was seen as glaring and perhaps was thus deftly closed up at the urging of Weik, drawing on probability.

36 "Now that they were"—Herndon, *Life,* 112.

36 "But the ghost of another"—Herndon, *Life,* 112.

36 "woefully abstracted"—Herndon, *Life,* 113. Same for the other quotation in this paragraph.

37 "There is no question"—Herndon, *Life,* 114.

38 Reburial of Ann Rutledge—Details of the exhumation and transfer of Ann's body are taken from the lengthy and well-researched 1969 article in the *Lincoln Herald* by Gary Erickson.* The fact that a nameplate was found in the grave was specifically recalled by a friend of Montgomery (Erickson, 97), a claim, of course, now beyond testing. Doubts have been expressed about the existence of this nameplate but there seems no good reason why even on the frontier a plain, perhaps makeshift identity marker might not have been affixed. Today the old Concord Burial Ground, while unchanged, is kept clear of undergrowth and is enclosed by a chain-link fence. Over the former site of Ann's grave stands a simple wooden sign announcing, "This marks the original grave of Ann Rutledge, born Jan. 7, 1813 and died Aug. 25, 1835." Judging by the dates on the remaining headstones, when Lincoln went there to visit Ann's grave during the fall of 1835, and perhaps later, the cemetery could not have held more than a dozen burials in all. Since her brother's headstone, just to the right, was not put up until 1842, when Lincoln saw her grave it would have been set off by itself, occupying the top of the rise.† Seldom visited now, mostly screened from the few surrounding roads by a huddle of tall trees, silent except for the sound of wind and birds, the spot is still difficult to reach, requiring a long trek over hilly fields.

39 The Masters verse on Ann's headstone—line eight omits the phrase "in life" to be seen in all printings of the poem, and line two ends with an exclamation point rather than the usual colon. Since Masters was living when the stone was cut (1921) he may have made the changes himself.

Chapter 3: Wavering Memories

40 "He is a dirty dog"—Turner, 415. Same for the other quotations in this paragraph. Mary's assertion that Lincoln told her she was "the only woman he ever cared for" is no doubt true and of course could have been sincerely meant. It does appear, however, that he never bothered to tell her about Mary Owens (see chapter 8) and probably not about Ann. But in such matters who can tell? And of course it would make no great difference whether he had or hadn't. Lincoln and Mary first met in 1839, when Ann had been dead for five years and when Mary Owens back in Kentucky was preparing to marry another man. It is interesting, even more than

---

*Montgomery himself, in 1921, made a detailed affidavit on the exhumation, from which Erickson quotes. The boy who was present, James Hollis, then aged about nine, also later gave some details.

†It lay unmarked until the returned McNamar set up a board at its head bearing her initials (see p. 168). Whether this was done while Lincoln was going there is unknown.

somewhat intriguing, to note that twenty years later Lincoln's son Robert contradicted his mother (then dead), taking a different view about Ann. In the massive "official" biography of his father by Nicolay and Hay, written under his strict control, he allowed a brief yet surprisingly strong statement in support of the legend. At New Salem, wrote Nicolay and Hay, Lincoln "had become much attached to a young girl named Ann Rutledge, the daughter of one of the proprietors of the place. She died in her girlhood, and though there does not seem to have been any engagement between them, he was profoundly affected by her death" (I, 191–92). Of even greater interest in this regard is another fact, one that has received very little if any direct comment. Nicolay, a decade later, when preparing a one-volume edition of the ten-volume original work, quietly expanded on that brief passage. Rather unexpectedly, he now gave a full-page description of the romance, putting entire credence in the Herndon version, though without naming Lincoln's old partner (*Short Life*, 54). Any link Robert may have had to this longer version has gone unrecorded. Nevertheless, it is very difficult to believe that Nicolay would have taken the action without his approval. What it was that convinced him, if anything beyond the New Salem testimony by then available in the books of Lamon, Herndon, and Tarbell, cannot now be said. That Robert had, years earlier, tried to mute Herndon's propagation of the legend (see, for instance, Donald, 230–31) is hardly germane, since he was acting on behalf of his outraged mother.

40 "foul aspersions"—*Chicago Tribune,* March 6, 1867, as reprinted in *New York Times,* March 9, 1867. Same for the other quotations in this paragraph. Smith's long letter to Herndon of Jan. 24, 1867, is preserved in the Herndon-Weik Papers, reel 9-1410. On its margins in Herndon's hand are penciled two comments. The first reads: "Foolish. This man left a bad character here" (Donald, 237, quotes this as "base character," but "bad" is correct). The second reads: "Knows nothing of Lincoln. Smith gave Lincoln a bust of his. Lincoln never condescended to write his name on it." For further on the Smith-Herndon exchange see Donald, 236–38.

41 "that his heart was"—*Chicago Tribune,* March 7, 1867, as reprinted in *New York Times,* March 10, 1867. "It is to be regretted," commented the anonymous *Tribune* writer, "that such a story was ever made public, and more so that it was not put at rest at the time it made its appearance."

42 "too highly colored"—Arnold, 42.

42 "dripped from him as"—Herndon, *Life,* 473.

42 Nancy Rutledge Prewitt—The interview, conducted at Mrs. Prewitt's home in Fairfield, Iowa, appeared in *Chicago Inter-Ocean,* Feb. 12, 1886. There was some reprinting of the article, but it is hard to decide how widely. Concerning possible photographs of Ann, the daguerreotype process

was not made public, originally in France, until 1839 and was not put to use in this country until the following year. Josephine Chandler of Petersburg was one who thought she had actually seen a photograph of Ann, apparently about 1895: "I remember a hot afternoon in my late teens when 'Aunty Hill'—the Mrs. Samuel Hill of New Salem days—told me the story of Ann Rutledge, and showed me old daguerreotypes of herself and Ann (which last now seems to have disappeared)" (Chandler, 503). Could Parthena Hill have shown her, rather than an original daguerreotype, some sort of painting or sketch that had later been photographed? No claim presently exists regarding pictures of Ann, of any kind.

43 "when the tragic death"—Tarbell, *Early*, 222.

43 "Could Lincoln sing?"—Hertz, 138.

44 "most careful examination"—Barton, *Women*, 185.

44 Sarah ("Sally") Rutledge Saunders—Her early contact with the New Salem restoration is recorded in Reep, 77, 98, 99; see also Hammand, 5–7. The pewter coffee pot and the family Bible she donated are still to be seen on exhibition, but the riding saddle, if it ever reached New Salem, is no longer to be found. The Rutledge family Bible, now on permanent exhibition, I was permitted to examine (I am grateful to Eileen Altig of the New Salem staff for arranging this). But it contains nothing beyond the entries in the family record section, which have been published, and the signatures of Ann's father and brother William. I had hoped to find a sample of Ann's own handwriting—based on some stray statements in a separate file at the Illinois State Historical Library asserting that Ann had noted several of her birthdays in the volume. Nothing appeared, disappointingly, though an extra sheet, now missing, had once been pasted to the opening page of the *Apocrypha* which could have held such writing. In a letter written a year before her meeting with Barton, Sarah mentioned the only specific memory she had of her sister: "I remember seeing her about her household duties and that I once sat on a low stool at her feet while she was working with her needle, that she stopped her work and threaded my needle for me and gave me my first lesson in sewing" (Hammand, 6.) This memory of Ann is especially appropriate, for several people recalled her reputation as an expert needlewoman.

45 The Barton interview with Sarah Saunders—Quotations in the text are from the printing of the syndicated story in *San Diego Sun,* Jan. 11, 1922 (clipping at the Lincoln Library, Ft. Wayne). Curiously, in the syndicated story there is no mention of David Rutledge's letter to his father with its postscript to Ann. The official unveiling of that document was reserved for a talk Barton gave at the restored New Salem in May 1926, in which he explained, "it was placed for a time in my hands by the last surviving sister of Ann Rutledge . . . with the privilege of use" (Barton, "Salem," 82–83). A

letter written by her son James to George Hambrecht in March 1922 describes Sally's condition at the time of the Barton interview: "At times her mind partially fails her and she becomes somewhat forgetful of her surroundings, but this soon passes away and then she talks with her usual ability" (Hambrecht Papers, Wisconsin Historical Society, Madison). That Sally stayed mentally vigorous in her old age may be seen in an unpublished letter she wrote with her own hand in May 1919 commenting on a then recent novel about her sister (*The Soul of Ann Rutledge*, by Bernard Babcock, Lippincott, Philadelphia, 1919): "I want to thank you for sending the Book but I am sorry there is so many mistakes in it My Father's name was James not John. Then there is no truth in that quilting B neither of them would stoop to such .things. . . . there was not any of that kissing between them & there is a lot more that is not true at all. So if anyone asks you about the Book tell them I know what I am talking about" (from the original at the Illinois State Historical Library).

46 The McNamar farm in Sandridge was purchased by him in July 1832 (Reep, 105), and the Rutledge family moved from New Salem to occupy it some six months later. This was done at the invitation of McNamar in anticipation of his marriage to Ann, or so it has been believed. But McNamar, in writing Herndon in 1867, said, "I intended it for a home for my Father's family, intending myself to pursue the Mercantile Business. . . . The Rutleges were induced to occupy and take care of the place by my friend and agent Dr. Allen" (Jan. 20, 1867, Herndon-Weik Papers, reel 10). This aspect of the story, it appears, is destined to remain clouded.

48 "Neither Ann nor Abraham"—Beveridge, 150.

48 "No one in New Salem"—Barton, *Women*, 180.

49 The Marsh letter—Barton did not actually discover this document, but he was allowed first use of it by the owner, the collector Oliver Barrett, who had purchased it some unknown time before, presumably from Marsh's descendants. The original manuscript of the survey Lincoln did for Marsh was also supplied by Barrett. (Barton, "Salem," 82).

49 For Barton's excessively negative opinion of McNamar, see *Women*, 173–84. His attitude may have also been influenced by the 1916 book by Henry Rankin, who as a young man in the 1870s was well acquainted with McNamar. "I knew him the last ten or 12 years of his life," stated Rankin, "as intimately as any young man could know an elderly man of so cold and unsocial a nature as his. I respected and admired him both for his ability as an accountant and as a skillful examiner of land titles. . . . [His] marriage the year after he returned to New Salem showed he was not inconsolably grieved by the early death of the good and charming Ann" (Rankin, 69). He also quotes McNamar's second wife as saying, "There

was no more poetry or sentiment in him than in the multiplication table" (70), which seems overdone, as do Rankin's own comments. As a young man, McNamar, it is known, read Shakespeare, Pope, Cervantes, and Burns, owning copies of all these works (letter, Nov. 26, 1866, Herndon-Weik Papers, reel 8-1129). An additional and really unavoidable thought on the topic of McNamar's supposedly dour personality is this: why may not *his* temperament too, as well as Lincoln's, have been somewhat altered by the shock of Ann's death? In his case, in a way, hearing of his loss all at once on the day of his arrival back at New Salem, the fact could have struck with even more peculiar impact than it had Lincoln. If so, the difference in the reaction of the two personalities is revealing. To Lincoln, ultimately, it gave depth, but to McNamar, apparently only bitterness. For further detail bearing on the question, see pp. 136 and 168.

49 "into the face"—Sandburg, 81. Same for the other quotations in this paragraph.

50 "or from one-time"—Angle, "Love," 6. Same for the other quotations in this paragraph.

50 "entertains no doubt of"—Angle, "Love," 7.

51 The Minor Affair—The fullest exposition of this episode is in the Fehrenbacher pamphlet of 1979. Even there, however, the whole story is not given, especially regarding the perpetrators who seem to have melted from the scene, admitting nothing and leaving no trace. See also Angle's article in *Atlantic Monthly* and newspapers of the time. Another, less ambitious Lincoln-Rutledge hoax of an earlier time, a crude attempt not worth pursuing, was the production of a stone with the names of Abe and Ann and the date of their betrothal supposedly scratched in. (This one, it seems, roped in the collector Oliver Barrett.) Rather than surprise that there should be such underhanded attempts to cash in on the legend, it is cause for wonder that there have not been many more of them, and more successfully done.

52 "consigned the Ann Rutledge"—Neely, 265. The article adds with some overstatement: "The romance is now regarded as unproved, and its profound effect on Lincoln's life as completely disproved." The overstatement is that "completely."

52 "essential results"—Randall, 341. Same for the other quotations in this paragraph.

53 "not for any intrinsic"—Randall, 321.

53 "Here is one person reporting"—Randall, 328.

53 "artificial and made to"—Randall, 335. Same for the other quotations in this paragraph.

54 "In its origin the Ann"—Randall, 339.

54 Some of the leading negative and even hostile treatments of the

Rutledge legend, before and after Randall, may be read in the following: Basler, *Legend,* 147–62; Donald, 218–41; Lewis, *Libel,* 85–100; Masters, 45–61; Randall, *Mary,* 395–407; Ross, *Wife,* 269–83; Warren, "Myth" and "Ghost." In the two best-known single-volume biographies of Lincoln—those by Benjamin Thomas (1952) and Stephen Oates (1977)—Ann is rather summarily dismissed. As Thomas viewed it, the legend rested on "a mass of contradictory evidence" supplying at best "a frail frame of reality" that has been firmly rejected by most competent scholars as "improbable" (*Biography,* 49–51). Oates, even more briefly, concludes that Lincoln's garrulous New Salem neighbors "spawned legends" about the romance but that there existed "no evidence that Ann and Lincoln ever had anything more than a platonic relationship" (19).

55 "Available evidence"—Simon, "Rutledge," 33. Simon concludes forth-rightly that Ann "simply will not go away.... She should take her proper place in Lincoln biography."

55 "reclassified the romance"—Simon, "Rutledge," 27. Same for the other quotations in this paragraph.

55 "because Cogdal asked"—Simon, "Rutledge," 26.

56 The three questions—Wilson, "Evidence," 309–12.

56 "at first shied away"—Wilson, "Evidence," 312.

57 "was not an obscure"—Wilson, "Evidence," 317.

Chapter 4: She Had an Angel's Heart

All quotations in this and the following three chapters, except in one instance, are from the original letters to Herndon and from his interview notes, all preserved in the Herndon-Weik Papers at the Library of Congress (microfilm reels 7 through 12). For the backgrounds of the witnesses see the entries in Miller, Onstot, and Reep, along with the specific sources named. Reel citations, below, itemize documents by number.

59 "He at this time fell"—Letter, May 29, 1865, reel 7-39.

60 "Miss Rutledge had auburn"—Herndon, *Life,* 107. For this undated quote from Mrs. Bale the manuscript is missing. Herndon's text specifies that Mrs. Bale knew Ann personally. For Lincoln giving advice to Abram Bale, see the Bale pamphlet, 16–17.

61 "He was studious—so much"—Letter, May 29, 1865, reel 7-73. For Graham's background, see the biography by Duncan and Nickols (unfortunately marred by fictionalizing and by unidentified speculation). The book also claims far too much by calling its subject "The Man Who Taught Lincoln." From the evidence, the most that can be said is that Graham was one of the men Lincoln went to for help when he needed to have something in his studies explained. The quoted passage is also given by Duncan and Nickols, 252, but in a badly garbled form.

61 William G. Green—The extent to which Lincoln's helper at the New Salem store and mill, Billy Green, prospered after leaving the village has never been well understood. Too often today's writers have been content to tag him with a spurious nickname ("Slicky Bill"), which is suggested in only a single, evidently prejudiced source (Onstot) not otherwise well attested and by supplying vague references to a later business career. (The nickname occurs in only one other primary source that I have seen, an unpublished letter of John Hill to Ida Tarbell, Feb. 17, 1896, Tarbell Papers, Allegheny College, Meadville, Pa.) In reality, among all the pioneers of central Illinois, Green was one of the most successful, reaching a net worth of over a half million dollars (Miller, 714) and even gaining a measure of political influence in the state, as well as in banking and railroading. He and his wife raised one daughter and eight sons, three of whom fought for the Union in the Civil War. In his late seventies his legs for some reason became paralyzed, and he was confined to a wheelchair. He died in 1894. His relations with Lincoln are well covered in the literature: in addition to Reep, Onstot, and Miller, see in particular Herndon, Lamon, Tarbell, and Thomas, *Salem;* also a pamphlet, *Biographical Sketch of William Green of Menard County,* by J. R. Williams (Brink Co., 1874), and the *Biographical Encyclopedia of Illinois in the Nineteenth Century* (Galaxy, Philadelphia, 1875). Later he spelled his name Greene.

62 Green's visit to the White House is variously reported (see Tarbell, *Life,* 140). The only other New Salemite, apparently, to visit Lincoln as president was Charles Maltby, who as a youth had helped out at Lincoln's two New Salem stores and at the grist mill (Shutes, *California,* 221–23). There may have been other New Salem neighbors who went to see their old friend in Washington, but these two are the only ones reliably reported. Maltby later, while living in California, wrote a short biography of Lincoln (1884), unfortunately saying little about his own recollections of his subject. Residing at New Salem for about a year and a half during 1831–33, he remarks only that "the writer has pleasant memories of the days and nights spent with Lincoln in the log store. . . . Many were the evenings in which our thoughts and conversation turned to our boyhood days, and to a recital of the incidents and experience of our childhood. Those reminiscences of Lincoln . . . are treasured up as pleasant memories" (Maltby, 27). Not one of those memories does he provide, however, and his brief biography is made up of material taken from the standard sources.

62 The Lincoln-Armstrong match—Green's brief but basic description of this encounter is found in his 1860 interview with J. Q. Howard (Basler, "Notes," 399; the printing of the Howard notes in Mearns, 154, omits a small but significant portion). My description of the bout gives the action as Green saw it, modified by several other references: Howells, 34; Reep, 25–26; and letters to Herndon from James Short (July 7, 1865), Row

Herndon (July 3, 1865), Lynn Green (July 30, 1865), Henry McHenry (Oct. 10, 1866); also an interview with Royal Clary (Basler, "Notes," 394).

63 "He in the years 1833"—Letter, May 30, 1865, reel 7-90. The Herndon-Green correspondence involved a dozen letters from Green, but there is no more about Ann.

64 "Yours of yesterday is"—Letter, June 6, 1865, reel 7-116. Somehow, all knowledge of the *Axis* article was lost until 1944, when it was uncovered by Jay Monaghan, who reported on it that fall in the *Abraham Lincoln Quarterly*. For an idea of the excitement generated see the commentary by Lloyd Lewis in the *New York Times* on Feb. 11, 1945. The original of the *Axis* clipping sent by Hill to Herndon is still with his letter. My quotation in the text is from a copy of the original paper on file at the Illinois State Historical Library, Springfield, dated Feb. 15, 1862.

65 *Talisman*—This experiment at opening the Sangamon to mercantile traffic is well covered in the literature. See in particular Beveridge, Pratt, *"Talisman,"* and Thomas, *Salem*. On the Sangamon River today at the restored New Salem a reproduction of the *Talisman* offers rides to visitors.

66 "You ask about him"—Letter, July 3, 1865, reel 7-218.

67 "When I arrived there"—Flindt. This passage in the original interview was omitted from reprints of the article that I have seen. The death of Row Herndon's wife is also mentioned in Reep, 45, and Onstot, 150. ("He acquired some notoriety by shooting and killing his wife. Whether accidental or on purpose the people were about equally divided in their opinions. He was fooling with a loaded gun and it went off and killed her." If Onstot had known that Nancy Rutledge was in the Herndon cabin when the gun went off he might have been slower to mention the gossipy rumor about a deliberate shooting.) There were no follow-up stories in the *Journal* to its brief initial account of the accident. It is possible that Lincoln himself wrote the short *Journal* account or at least reported the facts. As is known, the paper's editor, Simeon Francis, was his close friend, and Lincoln did contribute to the paper, though perhaps not this early.

68 James Short—For Short's buying up the Lincoln surveying equipment see Reep, 65, 103, and Thomas, *Salem*, 110. Short's residence at Sandridge is mentioned in Miller, 377, and Reep, 124, where the date of Short's marriage is also given. In later life Short went to California, where he was appointed an Indian agent by President Lincoln. Of all the men Lincoln knew during his youth, Short in some ways seems to have made the deepest impression on him. "I have known him to be as honorable a man as there is in the world," he said later (Lincoln, *Works*, I, 81).

70 "Mr. L. boarded with"—Letter, July 7, 1865, reel 7-227. In April 1866 Herndon spoke with Short, but the brief note he made has no mention of Ann, referring only to Lincoln and the Armstrong family.

71 "As to the condition of"—Letter, Jan. 1, 1866, reel 7-273.

72 Miles's letter to Herndon—Mar. 23, 1866, reel 8-681. The letter opens: "In answer to yours of the 19th I have to say that the references you gave me knew little or nothing of what you wanted to know. So I called on the old women whose heads are always clear and recollection good Especially on matters of courtship in early life." It ends with this fitting comment: "If you should undertake to write a history of my life after I am dead I don't want you to inquire so close into my early courtships as you do of Mr. Lincoln." If nothing else, that wry remark helps in the appreciation of Herndon's dedication in research. Today, as inheritors of the full-blown Lincoln legend, we could wish he had done more. But in his own day it appeared to many that his constant, insistent probing verged on the fanatic.

73 Parthena Hill and Ann Rutledge—That these two were *best* friends is my own interpretation of the evidence, but that they were close is certain. Mrs. Hill, who while single lived with her family at nearby Farmer's Point, later recalled that Ann often traveled from New Salem to visit her: "came out to my father's house saw her frequently—knew her well" (interview, 1887, notes, reel 11-2861). Josephine Chandler, whose own roots were deep in the New Salem–Petersburg area, recalled a visit about 1895 with "Aunty Hill," during which the old lady talked feelingly of Ann, showing pictures and "from a precious old reliquary produced a scrap of 'bottle-green' flannel from which cloth the two friends, when girls, had riding habits in duplicate" (Chandler, 503). For some comment on the "daguerreotypes" shown by Mrs. Hill, see p. 151. It is also sufficiently clear that Ann shared with her friend Parthena at least one letter, a crucial one, she received from John McNamar (see pp. 135, 167).

Chapter 5: Lincoln Told Me So

See the headnote to chapter 4.

74 John McNamar—Details of the first contact between Miles and McNamar are noted by Miles on McNamar's first letter to him, reel 8-750.

74 "I left here in 32"—Letter, May 5, 1866, reel 8-750.

76 "I received your very"—Letter, June 4, 1866, reel 8-750. For the date of Lincoln's return to New Salem from his war service, see Miers, 29. Somewhat complicating the question of just when McNamar left the village is a notice that appeared in the *Sangamon Journal,* Jan. 5, 1833:

Dissolution—The Co-partnership heretofore existing under the form of Hill & McNeal was, by mutual consent, dissolved on the 4th of September 1832. N.B. The Notes and accounts of the said firm are in the hands of

Bowling Green, Esq., where those interested are solicited to call—he being
fully authorized to settle the same.

Samuel Hill
John M'Neal

New Salem, Jan. 3, 1833

Whether this means that McNamar was still in New Salem on September
4, 1832, or perhaps had earlier signed a postdated instrument is hard to
say. Why publication of the action was delayed for four months is another
unanswerable question. The name McNeil was given several different
spellings.

78 "tolerably good schollar"—Notes, April 2, 1866, reel 8-696. Same
for the other quotations in this and the following paragraphs. (The printing
of this passage in Duncan and Nickols, 253, contains many small errors
and omissions).

79 "the first week he came"—Notes, Oct. 1866, reel 11-3000.

79 "a tall, good-looking man"—Onstot, 231. Same for the other quotation in this paragraph.

80 "Lincoln told Isaac Cogdal"—Letter, Aug. 27, 1866, reel 8-923.

80 "that he really did love"—Letter, June 22, 1866, reel 8-963.

81 Erastus Wright's recollections of his meeting with Lincoln as president-
elect were first published in 1927 (see the bibliography under "Wright").
So far as is known, his diary has been lost, so the precise date of his
meeting with Lincoln cannot be recovered.

81 "I think it was in 1859"—Cogdal to B. F. Irwin, April 10, 1874, first
published in the *Illinois State Journal,* May 15, 1874, reprinted in Rankin,
309-10, and Taggart, 310. Corroboration for Cogdal's claim in this letter
about Lincoln's talking religion with him is at hand in Herndon's notes of
another of his talks with Cogdal (undated but certainly 1866-67):

> I have often talked with Mr. Lincoln on the question of religion in his own
> office and in your presence too (This is true, Herndon). Mr. Lincoln believed
> in God and in all the great substantiating groundwork of religion.... He did
> not believe in Hell—Eternal punishment as the Christians say—His view
> was punishment as education.... I have battled this often and often with
> him commencing as early as 1834 and as late down as 1859 (This is
> correct Herndon)" (reel 11-3000b).

82 The Cogdal interview—Herndon's notes are written on both sides
of a single sheet of paper (reel 11-3000). The marginal note he made
concerning the manner in which Cogdal raised the crucial question with
Lincoln is on the reverse. Lamon, 169, in printing this interview quietly

inserts the marginal note into the text as if it occurred there naturally. Herndon, in *Life,* 389, gives the meeting more briefly, quoting Lincoln directly only when he speaks of Ann and not mentioning the added words. The true significance of the marginal note was first suggested by Douglas Wilson when he pointed out how it greatly enhanced "the credibility of such an answer" (Wilson, "Evidence," 316).

85 "if Mr. Lincoln was crazy"—Notes, undated, reel 11-3000b.

86 "in search of facts"—Herndon's lecture, 27. Same for the other quotations in this paragraph.

86 "I left behind me in"—Herndon, *Life,* 108. Same for the other quotations in this and the following paragraphs. The original notes of this conversation are missing, but it is clear that the passage in *Life* came out of this same October 1866 visit to the McNamar farm. In his book Herndon casts the words as being spoken by the just-departing McNamar directly to Ann.

87 "rapid filling up of"—Letter, Dec. 1, 1866, reel 8-1183. During my several visits to the old Concord Cemetery I was unable to find the grave of McNamar's mother. A number of the stones, however, have sunk almost out of sight.

87 "The cemetery contains"—Herndon's lecture, 10. When Herndon visited the Concord Cemetery in October 1866, to judge by the dates on those stones still legible, it was no longer receiving burials.

Chapter 6: The Rutledges Speak

See the headnote to chapter 4.

88 "Oh Mother dear, a short"—Wundram. Mrs. Rutledge is buried in Bethel Cemetery, Birmingham, Iowa, not far from the home in which she died and in which she had lived for nearly forty years after leaving Illinois.

89 "I have the honor to"—Letter, Aug. 5, 1866, reel 8-793. This is a response to Herndon's letter of July 30, 1866, which has not survived.

90 "Having been sent to"—Letter, Aug. 12, 1866, reel 8-803. Regarding Robert's position as provost marshal in Iowa during the war, the tradition is that Lincoln personally made the appointment. However, the records of the War Department at the National Archives mention only the recommendation of Rep. James Wilson of Iowa (Simon, "Rutledge," 26). The appointment was made on May 8, 1863.

90 "I fully appreciate"—Letter, Oct. 30, 1866, reel 8-996.

90 "Robert was here some"—Letter, Nov. 4, 1866, reel 8-1014.

91 "Believing that any"—Letter, Nov. 1866, reel 8-1343. Same for the two extracts that follow.

93 "As to the relation"—Letter, Oct. 22, 1866, reel 8-1358. That Robert was a visitor at the Jones house in Winterset, Iowa, at the time this letter was written is recorded in Robert to Herndon, Oct. 30, 1866: "I have just returned from Madison Co. some 200 miles west of this place & compared notes with John Jones formerly of Menard Co Ill, who fully corroborates my statement." Jones's own letter supports this, and it also appears to say that he has read Robert's long letter to Herndon of late November 1866: "Having seen the statements made by RB Rutledge in reference to the early life of Abraham Lincoln and having known Mr. Lincoln & been an eyewitness to the events as narrated from my boyhood, I take pleasure in saying they are literally true."

94 "bold, manly, & substantially"—Letter, Nov. 18, 1866, reel 8-1050. Same for the quotation in the following paragraph.

95 "Ann told me once"—Letter, Nov. 21, 1866, reel 8-1073. Same for the other quotations in this and the following two paragraphs.

96 "She was a beautiful girl"—Pond, "Memoirs," 9. Twenty years later Herndon did manage to speak with him, but nothing new or significant resulted (notes, reel 14-1494).

96 "I had the honor to"—Pond, "Memoirs," 11.

96 Jean Rutledge Berry—That Ann's elder sister, also called Jane, left an independent record of the romance that predated Herndon has not before been mentioned. Tarbell (*Early*, 218) says merely that Jean's statement "has been preserved in a diary kept by the Rev. R. D. Miller, now Superintendent of Schools of Menard County, with whom she had the conversation." Probably Tarbell did not know that Jean had died at her home in Rock Creek on August 24, 1866, well before there was any exchange of information between Herndon and the Rutledges. Miller later produced two versions of his work on local history, the first in 1879. In this, in speaking of the romance he refers only to a few "old settlers" (208) as his sources, not mentioning Jean. Ten or so years later he allowed Tarbell to see his diary, from which she quoted in her *McClure's* article of 1895. In the second version of his county history, published in 1905, Miller also says that his information came from a few old settlers, but he adds, "and especially from old 'Aunt Jane Berry' a younger sister of Anna Rutledge" (Miller, 20).

97 "With much embarisment"—Letter, Nov. 25, 1866, reel 8-1133. Herndon, *Life*, 112, quotes another letter from John of the same date but which is so similar to this one that it seems a garbled or edited version: "I have heard Mother say that Anne would frequently sing for Lincoln's benefit. She had a clear, ringing voice. Early in her illness he called and she sang a hymn for which he always expressed a great preference. It begins: 'Vain man, thy fond pursuits forbear.' You will find it in one of the standard hymn books. It was likewise the last thing she ever sung." Note

that the reference to Ann's "ringing voice" occurs only here, and that the undoubted version has her singing the hymn *before* she fell ill. John's quotation of the opening stanza of the standard hymn, usually called "Death," is very close to the original (see Lair, 11).

98 The modern Ann Rutledge was originally from Ottumwa, Iowa. A year earlier she had caused another little stir by enrolling as a student at Lincoln Memorial University in Tennessee, though remaining only a short time (*Lincoln Herald,* Feb. 1938). She was also a featured guest that year at a gala function held at the restored New Salem.

Chapter 7: A Parade of Witnesses

See the headnote to chapter 4.

99 Lynn McNulty Green—Letter, July 30, 1865, reel 7-267. Along with his brother William, David Rutledge, and William Berry, Lynn Green was one of four New Salem boys to attend college, the four going together to Jacksonville. Onstot, 140, says that he married a daughter of the Abells (see p. 120) and that "they had a boy named Johnny who was as small as Tom Thumb, & for years exhibited him on the road. Johnny was smart and a great favorite with the people." A second letter from Lynn adds only a brief description of Ann that makes her considerably more robust than the slight figure recalled by all the others: "She was of medium height, plump & round in form weighed 150 lbs. eyes blue not large. Hair a golden yellow—modest and unassuming in bearing about 22 years old without property."

100 George Spears—For Lincoln's letter, see Lincoln, *Works,* I, 25. Spears's letter is dated Nov. 21, 1866, reel 8-1080. A copy of the lecture was sent him by Herndon three days earlier. The quotation in the following paragraph is from this same letter.

100 Caleb Carman—Notes, Oct. 12, 1866, reel 8-979, and letter, Nov. 30, 1866, reel 8-1167. On exhibition at the restored New Salem is a chair from the old Carman cabin, well attested, with a cane seat that was supposedly once repaired by Lincoln. Carman said he boarded Lincoln "when he went to the legislature in 1834."

101 Jason Duncan—The manuscript consists of a six-page statement on various aspects of Lincoln's early life, without heading or date, followed by a brief note addressed to Herndon, also undated, reel 11-3014. It is clear that Duncan had read the November lecture, however, and this helps date the manuscript as probably of early 1867. Duncan was the man credited by Lincoln himself with introducing him to the William Knox poem "Mortality" (Carpenter, 60), but there is no mention here of that incident. Another resident of New Salem, Daniel Burner, affords a case similar to

that of Duncan. Though he knew Lincoln well at New Salem, Burner later flatly denied the link with Ann: "Talking about girls, I want to say there is no truth in the story about Lincoln being engaged to Ann Rutledge. On the other hand she was engaged to a man named McNeil, who was in the dry goods business there. One day he went east, it was supposed to buy goods, and never came back" (Temple, 69, quoted from an interview with the aged Burner in *Chicago Sunday Tribune,* Feb. 10, 1895). Burner himself admits to having left New Salem for good with his family as early as the spring of 1834, only some eight or nine months after McNamar's own departure. Of course that was well before Lincoln could have had any serious thoughts about marriage to Ann. That Burner heard nothing subsequently is indicated by his apparent ignorance of McNeil's pseudonym.

102 Henry Hohimer—Notes, Oct. [no year], reel 11-2976. Hohimer's age is noted as eighty-one in the notes, but his birthdate is not available.

102 B. F. Irwin—Letters, Aug. 27, 1866, and Sept. 22, 1866, reel 8-836.

103 William McNeely—Letters, Nov. 12, 1866, reel 8-1034, and Nov. 22, 1866, reel 8-1143.

104 William Bennett—Letter, no date but 1866, reel 11-2976. For the Godbey incident see Herndon, *Life,* 92. Lincoln's first survey of record, dated January 1834, was done for Godbey (Herndon, *Life,* 100).

105 Lizzie Bell—Notes, no date but 1887, reels 11-2973, 11-3083. At the top of his page of notes Herndon has scribbled: "Both father and daughter cranky—flighty—at times nearly non co[m]pus mentis—but good and honest." Mrs. Bell died shortly after the interview, in January 1888.

105 Harvey Ross—Portions of the Ross 1899 book were published earlier in various local newspapers. See, for instance, the *Fulton* (Mo.) *Democrat* of the 1890s (no more specific dates are at hand).

107 Arminda Rogers Rankin—For Lincoln's connection with the Rogers family of Athens, Illinois, see Rankin, 61–95 passim. See also the article by James Hickey, which is based on Hickey's discovery of a portion of the original Rogers library from the 1830s, including books purportedly used by Lincoln. For the quotation, see Rankin, 70–72.

108 Joshua Speed—Letter, dated at Louisville, Nov. 30, 1866, reel 8-1179. In the summer of 1841, some months after he wrote his letter to Dr. Drake, Lincoln paid an extended visit to Speed's home in Louisville. Dr. Drake at that time, in addition to his private practice, was serving as a professor at the Louisville Medical Institute (his tenure was 1839–46). Whether he and Lincoln met in that summer of 1841, or ever, is a question that may sometime be settled. A good deal has been written about Dr. Drake and his pioneering medical opinions, particularly in the field of social medicine: see the biography by Horine and the introduction

to Drake's own *Selected Writings.* Horine's article in *Manuscripts* ("Missing") indicates a wide and earnest search for additional letters to and from Dr. Drake, but with little success. He does not mention the Drake papers at the Wisconsin Historical Society (Draper Collection) containing letters to Drake, but they concern only the history of Cincinnati. Drake's high reputation in his own day is shown by the appearance, within three years of his death, of two lengthy books detailing his life and career (S. Gross, *A Discourse on the Life, etc.,* Louisville, 1853, and E. Mansfield, *Memoirs of the Life, etc.,* Cincinnati, 1855).

109 "You know I desired"—Lincoln, *Works,* I, 228.

110 "told me things which"—Dr. Henry to his wife, Feb. 18, 1863, original at the Illinois State Historical Library, Springfield. This file holds several other letters from Henry to his wife, but there is nothing further on the topic discussed here.

110 Dr. Henry—For biographical details see Pratt, "Dr. Anson G. Henry: Lincoln's Physician and Friend," *Lincoln Herald,* 45, Oct. 1943, 3–17; Dec. 1943, 31–40; also see Randall, *Marriage,* and Turner, for his association with the Lincolns, particularly the later years and following the assassination.

Chapter 8: The Matter of Mary Owens

111 The revelation of the Mary Owens story was Herndon's own doing, and he actually made a veiled reference to it in his Rutledge lecture. Talking of the Bennett Abell house at New Salem, he offered this tantalizing and now overlooked aside: "When the proper time comes I shall have to tell of another quite romantic love story that happened at this house" (Herndon's lecture, 16). Preoccupied by the Ann Rutledge sensation, none of his hearers or readers bothered to ask what he meant by this, and it was not until the Lamon book of 1872 that anything further was supplied about Mary. Herndon in his *Life* of 1889 added some detail, including the fact of Mary's death, then Mrs. Vineyard, in 1877.

111 "My little cabin on"—Letter, Feb. 15, 1867, reel 9-1448.

112 "intelligent and agreeable"—Lincoln, *Works,* I, 117.

112 "about one hundred fifty pounds"—Herndon, *Life,* 117.

112 "handsome, that is to say"—Lamon, 173.

112 "finer face"—Lincoln, *Works,* I, 118.

112 "not at all pleased"—Lincoln, *Works,* I, 118.

113 "get along through life"—Lincoln, *Works,* I, 118.

113 "with other things I"—Lincoln, *Works,* I, 54.

113 "Friend Mary, I have"—Lincoln's second letter to Mary is dated May 7, 1837, see Lincoln, *Works,* I, 78–79.

114 For the two incidents that annoyed Mary, see Herndon, *Life,* 120-21, where Mary confirms rumors of the first and herself describes the second. The hilly road involved in the first incident still exists. Now a blacktop, it leads from the former site of the Bowling Green cabin (just north of New Salem on the Petersburg road—site established by Rodney Dimmick of Petersburg), uphill west to the present location of Warburton's Restaurant, which stands approximately on the former site of the Abell cabin. Lincoln's party that day, which included Mrs. Green, was apparently on its way from one house to the other. When Bowling Green died suddenly of a stroke in 1842 he was at the Abell place, having just walked there from his own house at the foot of the hill (*Sangamon Journal,* Feb. 18, 1842). Henry Rankin as a youth was often in the Green home. For his warm memories of it, see his book, 49-50, 82.

115 Lincoln's letter to Mary of Aug. 16, 1837 (*Works,* I, 94-95), in its tone and its balanced coloration of phrase, deftly gives with one hand while taking with the other. No recipient of any intelligence could miss its message of rejection yet would be unable to pick out particular words or phrases as saying so much.

117 "scrape" . . . "word, honor"—Lincoln, *Works,* I, 119. The reference is to his later letter to the Brownings.

117 "I thought Mr. Lincoln"—McMurtry, "Appendix," 202.

118 "although I had seen her"—Lincoln, *Works,* I, 118. The reference is to his later letter to the Brownings.

119 Herndon's comments on the Abells are from his original manuscript draft of his Mary Owens chapter, reel 11-3464.

120 "He was always social"—Letter, Feb. 15, 1867, reel 9-1448.

120 "The courtship between him"—Letter, Feb. 15, 1867, reel 9-1448.

Chapter 9: His Heart in Her Grave?

123 The Marsh letter—This has been variously reprinted, in whole and in part, but the most accessible source is still Barton, "Lincoln." That Lincoln had his post office in the Hill store following the demise of his own store is very nearly certain (see Spears and Barton, 105-7, 131, and Thomas, *Salem,* 97).

123 For information on Charles Clarke and his letters home from New Salem in 1834-37 and from Petersburg in 1842-43, see Clarke, 559-81. He makes no mention of Lincoln, but once he comes close. In August 1834 he joined the crowd at a political rally near New Salem at which Lincoln, running for the second time and about to become a winner, would also have been present as one of thirteen candidates: "Our election takes place the first Monday in August. There is quite as much excitement

here as in N.H. on such occasions. I attended an old fashioned *Kentucky barbecue* last week for the benefit of candidates where they had feasting and drinking in the woods, the people behaved very well. There were many candidates present and each one made a stump speech."

124 "Timber land surveyed"—Barton, *Women,* 181.

125 "had no question in"—Barton, "Lincoln," 95.

125 Barton's interpretation of the Marsh letter was also rejected by one or two earlier commentators, though only in passing. Rather than disproving Lincoln's overwhelming grief, as one said, "it can just as readily be seen as supporting it" (Wilson, "Evidence," 320). Nor does the fact that Lincoln did a survey for Marsh a few days later really show an absence of grief in the surveyor. The task could easily have been pursued on a purely mechanical level—it would be interesting to see what might be revealed by a detailed study of that survey, if such were possible.

126 "was of a Drole singular"—Letter, July 3, 1865, reel 7-218.

126 "sort of loafer"—Logan, 2. The quotation in the footnote is from Chandler, 513. Hannah Armstrong's remark, as recalled by her son John, was not of course meant as criticism. It subtly expressed the usual countryman's approval of control and balance in a personality. Logan's use of the word, on the other hand, carried more than a hint of censure.

126 "While he was down there"—Logan, 3.

127 "The people of New Salem"—Notes, May 3, 1866, reel 8-732. Herndon too in his Rutledge lecture made an allusion to the alteration in Lincoln's personality, or perhaps it would be better to say temperament: "It may be, as alleged, that he was a warm, ardent and more or less impulsive man before 1835....His style and mode of expression in 1835 were entirely different from what they were [afterward]. He had more, much more emotion, fancy and imagination in 1835....Did this dread calamity, of which I have spoken, crush him and thus modify, if it did not change his nature?" (Herndon's lecture, 41–42).

127 "I always thought that"—Letter, Dec. 6, 1866, reel 8-1221.

127 "blackening with temporary"—Rankin, 93.

128 "a very modest and retiring"—Linder, 37.

128 "he did not make any"—Linder, 38–40.

129 "run off with all the talents"—Tarbell, *Early,* 29.

129 "seemed to run together"—Notes, undated, reel 7-335. See also Hertz, 353. Perhaps Herndon should not, even here, be blamed too much for his oversight. Mrs. Lincoln lived another four years after her stepson's death, dying at age eighty-one. In all that time, apparently, Herndon was the *only* investigator to seek her out for an interview. How much precious information about Lincoln's formative years, to say nothing of Ann, died with her!

130 *"An Interesting Relic"*—The quotation as given here is the whole text of the story as it appeared in the *Journal,* May 5, 1865. For Robert's brief note of correction, see *Journal,* May 9, 1865.

130 "the first branch of"—Howells, 29.

130 "a notion of studying"—Notes, signed by Graham, May 29, 1865, reel 7-77. Where Graham says he has "heard" that the book was then owned by the Rutledge family, it may only mean that he had read the story about the volume in the *Journal* of three weeks before (see two notes above). Five years earlier, while being interviewed for a campaign biography of Lincoln, Graham had mentioned the *Kirkham* volume in much the same fashion: "When L was about 22 [he] said he believed he must study Grammar—one could not be obtained in the neighborhood—walked 8 miles and borrowed Kirkham's old Grammar" (interviewer's notes, Mearns, 155). A point to be remembered about these early interviews of people in the New Salem–Petersburg area is this: all knew very well that *many* other old residents were still on hand to support or refute what any one of them might claim.

131 "I studied that very"—Flindt. During some ninety years after Ann's death the volume was carefully preserved in the Rutledge family, at different times in the possession of several members, including grandchildren. For a discussion of the book's provenance, and for some observations on the original book itself, see the appendix.

132 "One of those long"—Letter, Jan. 20, 1867, reel 9-1390.

132 Dr. Timothy Bancroft—Photographic copies of the two pages from his account book are at the Broome County Historical Society, Binghamton, N.Y. They were called to my attention by the society's former director, Marjory Hinman (in the same connection I am grateful for the assistance of Shirley Woodward, former Broome County historian). The original account book is in the possession of Dr. Bancroft's great-grandson, Paul Bancroft, of Lincoln, Nebraska. Since McNamar said that two others died besides his father, and the account book notes the death of George, then the third to die, sometime in late April or May 1833, was either David or Andrew. Location and verification of the father's tombstone in Coles Hill Cemetery (situated near West Colesville, just east of Binghamton and northwest of Windsor), was kindly accomplished for me by Minerva Flagg of Windsor, area historian, and Marjory Hinman. The headstone supplies only name, age, and date of death: "John Mcnamarah / Died April 10, 1833 / AE. 65 yr." For descriptions of the former New Ohio, N.Y. (at the present town of Tunnel), see H. P. Smith, *History of Broome County,* 1885, 339–41.

133 The exact site of the McNamara home, which was probably a farm, in New Ohio, Broome County, N.Y., has been lost. Apparently it was

"somewhere along the road between North Colesville and Harpursville, some sixteen miles northeast of Binghamton" (*Hamilton* [N.Y.] *Republican,* Feb. 8, 1945).

134 "got a letter from McNamar"—Notes, undated but 1886–87, reel 11-2861. The original passage from which the phrase in my text is quoted reads in full:

> Mr Hill told me that Ann's sickness was caused by her complications—2 engagements—She, Ann, did not hear of McNamar for a year or more—at last got a letter from McNamar telling her to be ready [inserted: "he having been engaged"] etc to be married—Lincoln who took advantage of McNamar's absence courted Ann—got her confidence etc & were in Mr Hill's & my opinion as well as the opinions of others that they were engaged—Ann thought that McNamar was playing off on her.

In the margin is penciled this further comment of Mrs. Hill: "I think that if McNamar got back from N.Y. before Ann's death that she would have married McNamar. I saw McNamar unload his furniture on arriving from N.Y. This is my honest opinion." Twenty years earlier, of course, she had said the opposite (see p. 73). Possibly, what she intends to say here is this: if McNamar had gotten back to New Salem *in good time,* say after a year away and before Lincoln made his move, then Ann's original feeling for him would have held. In the background of her belated contradiction may have been other obscure factors, for instance, her own husband having been one of Ann's rejected suitors.

135 "had overstaid his appointed"—Mrs. Hill to her son John, early February 1896, quoted in John Hill to Ida Tarbell, Feb. 6, 1896, original in Tarbell Papers, Alleghany College. The passage from Mrs. Hill's letter as quoted by her son reads in full (the two parenthetical statements are clarifications by John):

> I sent Feby No of McClure to my Mother at Petersburg Ills. In a letter today my mother has this paragraph—"I thank you for the magazine—I am sure the date is wrong about the year McNeil (John McNamar) sold out to your father and went East—He had just gone when we arrived here late in Oct. 1832. (This means the Nance family from Kentucky as emigrants). He came back after I went to housekeeping in 1835—late in the fall. He unloaded his furniture at Dr. Allen's just across the street from us, and one bedstead stood against the house for days, before it was taken in. He had written to Dr. Allen that his name was McNamar. I always thought Ann would have married him, if she had lived. He had overstaid his appointed time. Ann got a letter from him just before she took sick, saying, be ready—he would buy furniture in Cincinnati and wanted to be married as soon as he got here,

and go to housekeeping. I do not think I am mistaken in these dates." The underlining is in Mother's letter to me.

Further on, Hill's own portion of the letter has this: "Often heard Father tell of his having to lock Mr. Lincoln up in a room to prevent suicide after Ann Rutledge's death—Every effort was made to divert his mind—as a fact for a short time his mind wandered."

135 "it has ben very sickly"—Clarke, 566.

136 "unloaded his furniture"—See two notes above. Curiosity about why McNamar unloaded his wagon at Dr. Allen's place rather than at his own cabin in the village cannot now be satisfied. With him, of course, was his mother and several brothers and sisters, and there may be something to the fact that his own cabin had stood unoccupied for three years.

136 "never heard any person"—Letter, May 5, 1866, reel 8-750.

136 McNamar's placing a marker at Ann's grave was reported by himself: "While on the subject of graves I will mention that I cut the initials of Miss Ann Rutledge on a board at the head of her grave 30 years ago" (letter, Dec. 1, 1866, reel 8-1183). That he had, and kept, a lock of her hair is mentioned in another of his letters in which he describes finding a number of old Lincoln-related items: "Another discovery was a small Braid or Tress of Ann Rutledge's hair much worn and apparently moth eaten" (letter, Jan. 20, 1867, reel 9-1390). It appears he had specifically asked for the lock after being told of Ann's death on his return to New Salem. Nancy Rutledge in her 1886 interview with the *Inter-Ocean* recalled that "he protested his love for Annie, and begged my mother for some article that had been hers for a memento" (Flindt). That locks of hair were in fact taken from the dead girl was stated by Sarah Rutledge (see the Barton interview, p. 46).

137 "She was fair and her form"—Hickox. At this same interview occurred a fleeting comment by McNamar that should be recorded as showing his true feelings toward his old friend: "The mantle at McNamar's held a portrait of the President and 'Tad' looking over an album together, and on the wall in a decent frame hung the 'Proclamation' at which the old man kindled, saying: 'How well that reads. And the Inaugural—so peaceable and kind—so eloquent—make your hair stand right up.' " An obituary of McNamar appeared in the *Illinois State Journal,* March 3, 1879, which curiously manages to say little of his personal life. Only mentioned are his service as assessor and treasurer of Menard County, and the fact that he had been in business at New Salem. Concerning his part in the Rutledge legend the comment is almost offhand: "As the story runs, the fair and gentle Annie was originally John McNamar's sweetheart, but Abe took a 'shine' to the young lady and succeeded in heading off McNamar,

and won her affections. But Annie Rutledge died, and Lincoln went to Springfield."

137 "I can never forget"—Flindt.

137 "I am sorry to have"—Sarah Rutledge Saunders to George Hambrecht, March 18, 1922, copy in the Hambrecht Papers, Wisconsin Historical Society, Madison. The letter was written for her by her son James, who notes, "Mother's hand so trembled that she 'gave it up' and asked me to sign her name."

138 "never heard any"—Flindt. This of course may only show a disinclination to say much on the topic, but it probably also indicates that there was little contact between Lincoln and the Rutledge family at Sandridge immediately after Ann's death. Her brother Robert seems to admit as much in his comment to Herndon concerning the lecture: "You ask, secondly, do I get the condition of Mr. Lincoln's mental suffering and condition truthfully. I cannot answer this question from personal knowledge, but from what I have learned from others at the time, you are substantially correct" (letter, Nov. 21, 1866, reel 8-1073). Probably Robert's confession of ignorance indicates no more than that he did not get down to New Salem during the fall of 1835, thus did not encounter Lincoln when his grief was heaviest. But in talking to "others at the time" he did in fact hear of his friend's great "mental suffering."

139 The memory of Ann—That Lincoln would have tended to idealize Ann's memory needs no argument, especially linked as she was to the days of his youth. It is a common enough human trait. But that he was, at moments and to some degree, aware of the tendency in himself can be read in the lines of his own poem quoted as epigraph to this book. The dreamy visions of the midway world of memory, he wrote, appear "hallowed, pure, and bright" precisely because they have been "freed from all that's earthly vile." When he wrote those lines, Ann had been dead for perhaps a decade. That he may also have had others in mind—his mother and sister, obviously—does not lessen their force with regard to Ann.

Postscript

Some Additional Relics of Ann Rutledge
(see pp. 37–39, 149)

Late in March 1993, as this book was being readied for the press, there came to light unexpectedly in Springfield certain new relics of Ann Rutledge. In themselves of considerable interest, they also tend to complicate the picture of exactly what materials may have been found in Ann's grave at the exhumation of 1890.

Margaret Richardson, originally of Petersburg (a descendant of Jasper Rutledge, brother of McGrady Rutledge, Ann's favorite cousin and close friend), possesses several items that were supposedly removed from the coffin and withheld from the reburial. They have been in her family, she states, ever since they were given to her grandmother, a daughter of Jasper Rutledge and a namesake of the original Ann.*

Involved are four items: a small button, acorn-shaped, covered in cloth of faded rose; a bow, four inches wide, made of a grosgrain-like silky ribbon, perhaps originally white but now yellowish; a strip of black lace some two feet long and tapering to a point from a width of four inches; a lock of hair nearly two inches long by a quarter-inch thick (it matches the descriptions given by Ann's friends, light auburn or sandy).

Mrs. Richardson, who was born in Petersburg, has been aware of these relics since childhood, but vaguely, and without thinking them of great significance. She is unable to say how or why they were held out of the reburial in Petersburg's Oakland Cemetery, or by whom. But that they have in fact existed since that time is proved by a photograph of them that appeared in a booklet connected with the Chicago Columbian Exposition of 1893.† The caption in the booklet is very

---

*Jasper and McGrady were two of the twelve children of William Rutledge, brother of the original Ann's father, and his wife, Susannah.

†*Menard-Salem-Lincoln Souvenir Album*, edited and published by the Illinois Women's Columbian Club of Menard County, 1893 (reprinted in 1976 by Unigraphic Inc., Evansville, Ind.). Copies are at the Petersburg Historical Society and the Wisconsin Historical Society, Madison.

brief and gives no information beyond linking the items with Ann.

Since McGrady Rutledge was personally involved in the exhumation and reburial, most likely it was he who retained these things as mementos of his long-dead cousin. Then or later, he must have passed them to his brother Jasper, or directly to Jasper's daughter Ann. Why he did not preserve them in his own family, however, is a legitimate question: he had several daughters, one of whom was named Ann. Is it possible he gave away only *part* of what he took from the grave? At present, hundreds of Rutledges who might possess such relics are spread around the country, all descendants of the original Ann's parents and her aunts and uncles.

How these remains may fit with the enumeration of the coffin's contents obtained from other sources (see p. 149) is at least mildly puzzling. Would a burial dress have had buttons made of both cloth and pearl? (It was Ann's sister Nancy who specifically remembered the pearl buttons.) How could the large piece of black lace have been overlooked in earlier listings, and could such delicate material have survived fifty-five years in the ground? If these things, and perhaps others, were extracted from the coffin in 1890, then what besides the few bones and the hair is now in the box buried at Oakland Cemetery? Further complication sets in when it is realized that all the testimony on the subject relates to what was *found* in the coffin, not to what was reburied (see Erickson, 96–98).

The existence of Mrs. Richardson's collection was uncovered by John M. Sayre, of the Petersburg Historical Society, during a casual conversation with her son, Scott.* An earlier but passing encounter with it occurred in 1969, recorded by Erickson in his article. Obliquely, he refers to "a lady in Menard County who claims she has a lock of Ann's hair and a button from Ann's dress acquired from members of her family to whom they were given at the time of Ann's exhumation" (p. 97). His interest lapsed, apparently, when no authentication could be supplied (the lady in question, according to Mrs. Richardson, was her mother, then residing in Petersburg). The photograph of the collection (see second photo section) was made for this volume at the Herbert Georg Studio in Springfield.

---

*For bringing this matter to my attention I am grateful to Marianna Munyer, of the Illinois Historic Preservation Agency. For the discussion, I have drawn principally on Erickson; Reep; Pond; Barton; Onstott; Hertz; and Hammand (see the bibliography).

Selected Bibliography

Included here are all the published sources drawn on for the present study, as well as some whose contribution has been more general. Unpublished materials (original letters and notes in the Herndon-Weik Papers at the Library of Congress and other special documents) are identified at appropriate places in the notes. Except for a few special items, none of the fiction or drama connected with New Salem and Ann Rutledge is listed.

Angle, Paul, "Lincoln's First Love," *Bulletin, Abraham Lincoln Centennial Association,* 1 Dec. 1927.

———, "More Light on Lincoln and Ann Rutledge," *Bulletin, Abraham Lincoln Centennial Association,* 1 Sept. 1928.

———, "The Minor Collection: A Criticism," *Atlantic Monthly,* April 1929.

Anon., *New Salem: Official Catalogue,* State of Illinois, 1947.

Arnold, Isaac, *Life of Abraham Lincoln,* McClurg, Chicago, 1885.

Atkinson, Eleanor, *Lincoln's Love Story,* Doubleday, New York, 1909.

Bale, Ida, *New Salem as I Knew It* (pamphlet), Petersburg, 1939.

Baringer, William, *Lincoln's Vandalia,* Rutgers University Press, New Brunswick, 1949.

Barton, William, "Abraham Lincoln and New Salem," *Journal of the Illinois State Historical Society,* 19, 1926–27.

———, *The Women Lincoln Loved,* Bobbs-Merrill, Indianapolis, 1927.

Basler, Roy, *The Lincoln Legend: A Study of Changing Conceptions,* Houghton, Boston, 1935.

———, "J. Q. Howard's Notes on Lincoln," *Abraham Lincoln Quarterly,* 4, Dec. 1947.

———, *Collected Works of Abraham Lincoln.* See under *Lincoln.*

Baxter, M., *Orville Browning, Lincoln's Friend,* Indiana State University Press, Terre Haute, 1957.

Beveridge, Albert, *Abraham Lincoln 1809–1858,* Houghton, Boston, 1928.

Booton, Joseph, "New Salem Restoration," *Illinois Public Works,* Summer 1965.

Boritt, Gabor, *The Historians' Lincoln,* University of Illinois Press, Urbana, 1988.

Boyd, M. L., *William Knox and Abraham Lincoln: The Story of a Poetic Legacy,* Sage Books, Denver, 1962.

———, "Lincoln and the Influence of William Knox," *Lincoln Herald,* Spring 1958.

Brown, Marian, "Abraham Lincoln Capt," *Manuscripts,* Spring 1954.

Browning, Orville, *Diary 1850–1864,* Illinois State Historical Library, Springfield, 1925.

Carpenter, Frank, *Six Months at the White House,* Hurd, New York, 1866.

Chandler, Josephine, "New Salem: An Early Chapter in Lincoln's Life," *Journal of the Illinois State Historical Society,* Jan. 1930.

Clarke, Charles, "Sketch of Charles James Fox Clarke with Letters to His Mother," *Journal of the Illinois State Historical Society,* Jan. 1930.

Coleman, Charles, *Lincoln and Coles County,* Rutgers University Press, New Brunswick, 1955.

———, "Sarah Bush Lincoln, the Mother Who Survived Him," *Lincoln Herald,* Summer 1952.

Dall, Caroline, "Mr. Herndon's Account of Abraham Lincoln and Ann Rutledge," *Boston Daily Advertiser,* 15 Dec. 1866. Reprinted in *New York Times,* 16 Dec. 1866.

———, "Pioneering," *Atlantic Monthly,* April 1867.

Davis, J. M., "Lincoln as a Storekeeper and as a Soldier in the Black Hawk War," *McClure's,* Jan. 1896.

Donald, David, *Lincoln's Herndon,* Knopf, New York, 1948.

Duff, John, *Abraham Lincoln: Prairie Lawyer,* Rinehart & Co., New York, 1960.

Duncan, K., and Nickols, D., *Mentor Graham: The Man Who Taught Lincoln,* University of Chicago Press, Chicago, 1944.

Drake, Dr. Daniel, *Selected Writings.* See under *Shapiro.*

Ellenburg, N. C., *When New Salem Was New* (pamphlet), Petersburg, 1946.

Erickson, Gary, "The Graves of Ann Rutledge and the Old Concord Burial Ground," *Lincoln Herald,* Fall 1969.

Fehrenbacher, Don, *The Minor Affair: An Adventure in Forgery and Detection* (pamphlet), Lincoln Library, Ft. Wayne, 1979.

Flindt, Margaret, "Lincoln as a Lover [etc.], An Interview with Nancy, Sister of Ann Rutledge," *Chicago Inter-Ocean,* 12 Feb. 1886.

Gordon, J., "Abraham Lincoln in His Relations to Women," *Cosmopolitan,* Dec. 1894.

Hammand, Jane, *Memoirs of the Rutledge Family of New Salem, Illinois* (typescript, collects documents at the Library of Congress), 1921.

Harkness, D., *Lincoln's Favorite Poets,* Knoxville, 1921.

Herndon, William, *Lincoln and Ann Rutledge and the Pioneers of New Salem* (reprint of the original lecture of 1866), Trovillion Press, Herrin, Illinois, 1945.

———, *Herndon's Lincoln: The True Story of a Great Life,* Belford, Clark, Chicago, 1889. Reprinted by Da Capo Press, New York, 1983.

Hertz, Emmanuel, *The Hidden Lincoln: From the Letters and Papers of William Herndon,* Viking, New York, 1938.

Hickey, James, "Three R's in Lincoln's Education: Rogers, Riggin, and Rankin," *Journal of the Illinois State Historical Association,* Spring 1959.

Hickox, Volney, "Lincoln at Home: Reminiscences of His Early Life," *Illinois State Journal,* 15 Oct. 1874.

Holbert, G. K., "Lincoln and Linder in Illinois," *Lincoln Herald,* Oct.–Dec. 1942.

Holland, Josiah, *Life of Abraham Lincoln,* Gurdon Bell, Springfield, 1866.

Horine, E. F., *Daniel Drake, Pioneer Physician of the Midwest,* Pennsylvania State University Press, State College, 1961.

———, "Daniel Drake and the Missing Lincoln Letter," *Manuscripts,* Winter 1957.

Houser, M. L., "Some Books That Lincoln Read," in *Lincoln's Education and Other Essays,* Bookman Associates, New York, 1951.

Howells, W. D., *Life of Abraham Lincoln* (reprint of 1860 edition), Indiana University Press, Bloomington, 1960.

Kincaid, R., *Joshua Speed, Lincoln's Friend,* Lincoln Memorial University, Harrogate, 1943.

Lair, John, *Songs Lincoln Loved,* Duel, Sloan, New York, 1954.

Lamon, Ward Hill, *Life of Abraham Lincoln, from His Birth to His Inauguration as President,* Osgood, Boston, 1872.

Lewis, Lloyd, *Legends That Libel Lincoln,* Rinehart, New York, 1946.

———, "New Light on Lincoln's One Romance," *New York Times Book Review,* 11 Feb. 1945.

Lincoln, A., *Collected Works,* ed. Roy Basler, Rutgers University Press, New Brunswick, 1953.

Linder, Usher, *Reminiscences of the Early Bench and Bar of Illinois,* Legal News Co., Chicago, 1879.

Logan, Stephen, "S. T. Logan Talks about Lincoln," *Bulletin of the Lincoln Centennial Association,* 1 Sept. 1928.

Luthin, Reinhardt, *The Real Abraham Lincoln*, Prentice-Hall, New York, 1960.

McMurtry, R. G. [Mary Owens], Appendix, in *Lincoln's Other Mary* (fiction), by Olive Carruthers, Ziff-Davis, New York, 1946.

———, "Centre College, John Todd Stuart, and Abraham Lincoln," *Filson Club History Quarterly*, April 1959.

McNamar, Myrtle, *Gentle Ann: A Tale of the Sangamon* (versified fiction by the daughter-in-law of a son of John McNamar), Beacon, Boston, 1942.

Maltby, Charles, *The Life and Public Services of Abraham Lincoln*, Independent, California, 1884.

Masters, E. L., *Lincoln the Man*, Dodd, Mead, New York, 1931.

Mearns, David, *The Lincoln Papers*, Doubleday, New York, 1948.

Miers, Earl, *Lincoln Day-by-Day*, Lincoln Sesquicentennial Commission, Washington, 1960.

Miller, R. D., *Past and Present of Menard County, Illinois*, Clarke, Chicago, 1905. Revision of a section in *The History of Menard and Mason Counties*, Baskin, Chicago, 1879.

Minor, Wilma, "Lincoln the Lover," *Atlantic Monthly*, Dec. 1928, Jan., Feb. 1929 (the original Minor forgeries).

Mitgang, Herbert, *Lincoln as They Saw Him*, Rinehart, New York, 1956.

Monaghan, Jay, "New Light on the Lincoln-Rutledge Romance," *Abraham Lincoln Quarterly*, Sept. 1944.

Neely, Mark, Jr., *The Lincoln Encyclopedia*, Da Capo, New York, 1982.

Nelson, G., "The Genesis of Restored New Salem," *Journal of the Illinois State Historical Society*, Dec. 1943.

Newton, Joseph, *Lincoln and Herndon*, Torch Press, Iowa, 1910.

Nicolay, John, *A Short Life of Abraham Lincoln*, Century Co., New York, 1902.

Nicolay, J., and Hay, J., *Abraham Lincoln: A History*, Century, New York, 1891.

Oates, S. B., *With Malice toward None: The Life of Abraham Lincoln*, Harper, New York, 1977.

Onstot, Thomas, *Pioneers of Menard and Mason Counties*, Forest City, Illinois, 1902.

Pond, F. N., "The Memoirs of James McGrady Rutledge," *Journal of the Illinois State Historical Society*, April 1936.

———, *Intellectual New Salem in Lincoln's Day* (pamphlet), Lincoln Memorial University Press, Harrogate, 1938.

———, "Lincoln Lived Here," *Saturday Evening Post*, 15 Feb. 1941.

———. "Abraham Lincoln and David Rutledge," *Lincoln Herald*, June 1950.

Pratt, Harry, "Lincoln in the Black Hawk War," *Bulletin of the Abraham Lincoln Centennial Association,* Dec. 1938.

———, *The Personal Finances of Abraham Lincoln,* Abraham Lincoln Association, Springfield, 1943.

———, "Lincoln Pilots the *Talisman,*" *Abraham Lincoln Quarterly,* Sept. 1943.

Randall, James G., "Sifting the Ann Rutledge Evidence," in *Lincoln the President,* Dodd, Mead, New York, 1945.

Randall, Ruth, *Mary Lincoln: Biography of a Marriage,* Little, Brown, Boston, 1953.

Rankin, Henry, *Personal Recollections of Abraham Lincoln,* Putnam, New York, 1916.

Reep, Thomas, *Lincoln at New Salem,* Petersburg, 1927. Expanded from the original edition published by the New Salem Lincoln League, Petersburg, 1918.

Renne, Louis, *Lincoln and the Land of the Sangamon,* Chapman, Grimes, Boston, 1945.

Rennick, Percival, *Abraham Lincoln and Ann Rutledge, an Old Salem Romance* (pamphlet), a compilation of sources, 1932.

Ross, Harvey, *Early Pioneers and Pioneering Events in the State of Illinois,* Eastman, Chicago, 1899. Partial reprint as *Lincoln's First Year in Illinois,* Primavera Press, Elmira, N.Y., 1946.

Ross, Isabel, *The President's Wife: Mary Todd Lincoln,* Putnam, New York, 1973.

Sandburg, Carl, *Abraham Lincoln: The Prairies Years* (one-volume edition), Harcourt, New York, 1926.

Shapiro, H., and Miller, Z., eds., *Physician to the West: Selected Writings of Daniel Drake on Science and Society,* University of Kentucky Press, Lexington, 1970.

Shutes, M. H., *The Emotional Life of Abraham Lincoln,* Lippincott, Philadelphia, 1957.

———, *Lincoln and California,* Stanford University Press, Stanford, 1943.

Simon, John Y., "Abraham Lincoln and Ann Rutledge," *Journal of the Abraham Lincoln Association,* 11, 1990, 13–33.

Simon, Paul, *Lincoln's Preparation for Greatness: The Illinois Legislative Years,* Oklahoma University Press, 1965.

Spears, Z., and Barton, R., *Berry and Lincoln: The Store That "Winked Out,"* Stratford House, New York, 1947.

Speed, Joshua, *Reminiscences of Abraham Lincoln* (pamphlet), Louisville, 1884.

Stevens, F., *The Black Hawk War,* Chicago, 1903.

Strozier, Charles, "The Search for Identity and Love in Young Lincoln," in

Public and Private Lincoln, ed. C. Davis, Southern Illinois University Press, Carbondale, 1979.

Taggart, D. R., *The Faith of Abraham Lincoln,* Service Print Shop, Topeka, Kansas, n.d.

Tarbell, Ida, *The Early Life of Abraham Lincoln* (reprint of 1896 edition), Barnes, New York, 1974.

————. "Lincoln's First Love," *Collier's,* 8 Feb. 1930.

————, "Ann Rutledge," in *In the Footsteps of the Lincolns,* Harper Bros., New York, 1924.

Taylor, Richard S., *The Rutledge Tavern* (handbook, for use of guides), New Salem Village and Restoration, n.d.

Taylor, Richard S., and Johnson, Mark L., "Inventing Lincoln's New Salem: The Reconstruction of a Pioneer Village," unpublished paper given at the Illinois History Symposium, Springfield, Dec. 1992.

Temple, Wayne, "Lincoln and the Burners at New Salem," *Lincoln Herald,* Summer 1965.

Thomas, Benjamin, *Abraham Lincoln, a Biography,* Knopf, New York, 1952.

————, *Portrait for Posterity,* Rutgers University Press, New Brunswick, 1947.

————, *Lincoln's New Salem* (revision of 1934 and 1954 editions), Southern Illinois University Press, Carbondale, 1987.

Townsend, G. A., "A Talk with the Late President's Law Partner," *New York Tribune,* 8 Feb. 1867. Reprinted in *New York Independent,* 28 Feb. 1867.

Turner, Linda, *Mary Lincoln: Her Life and Letters,* Knopf, New York, 1972.

Warren, Louis, *Lincoln's Youth: The Indiana Years,* Indiana University Press, Bloomington, 1959.

————, "The Rutledge Ghost Stalks Again," *Lincoln Lore,* 8 March 1945.

————, "Herndon's Contribution to Lincoln Mythology," *Indiana Magazine of History,* Sept. 1945.

————, "The Ann Rutledge Myth," *The Lincoln Kinsmen,* May 1941.

————, "The Rutledge Family," *Lincoln Lore,* 15 Feb. 1932.

Weik, Jesse, *The Real Lincoln: A Portrait,* Houghton, Boston, 1922.

Whitney, H. C., *Life on the Circuit with Lincoln,* Estes & Lauriat, Boston, 1892.

Wilson, Douglas, "Abraham Lincoln and the Evidence of Herndon's Informants," *Civil War History,* Dec. 1990.

————, "William Herndon and His Lincoln Informants," unpublished lecture given at Lincoln Association Symposium, Springfield, 1991.

————, "Abraham Lincoln's Indiana and the Spirit of Mortal," *Indiana Magazine of History,* June 1991.

Wilson, R. W., *Lincoln among His Friends,* Caxton, Idaho, 1942.

Woldman, Harry, *Lawyer Lincoln,* Houghton, Boston, 1936.

Wright, Erastus, "Lincoln in 1831," *Bulletin of the Abraham Lincoln Association,* Dec. 1927.

Wundram, W., "Lincoln Called Her Mom" [Mrs. Rutledge], *Times-Democrat,* Iowa, 11 Feb. 1962.

Index

JOHN EVANGELIST WALSH has written some dozen scholarly books of history and biography covering a wide range of topics, from the Wright Brothers and St. Peter to John Paul Jones, Robert Frost, and Emily Dickinson. In articles he treats such subjects as Bible commentary, the Civil War, and Sherlock Holmes. His monograph *Poe the Detective: The Curious Circumstances behind the Mystery of Marie Roget* (1969) was awarded the nonfiction Edgar by the Mystery Writers of America. His pioneer study of the invention of the airplane, *One Day at Kitty Hawk* (1978), was selected by *Library Journal* for its list of the year's outstanding science-technical books and was condensed in *Reader's Digest*. Formerly a senior editor with several New York City book publishers, Walsh now writes full-time and is presently at work on a second Lincoln book, as well as a study of the Gospel of Mark. Father of four grown children, he lives with his wife, Dorothy, in Wisconsin.